Sean McManus

Web Design

6th edition

In easy steps is an imprint of In Easy Steps Limited
16 Hamilton Terrace · Holly Walk · Leamington Spa
Warwickshire · United Kingdom · CV32 4LY
www.ineasysteps.com

Sixth Edition

In Easy Steps Limited supports The Forest Stewardship Council (FSC),
the leading international forest certification organisation. All our titles
that are printed on Greenpeace approved FSC certified paper carry the
FSC logo.

MIX
Paper from
responsible sources
FSC® C020837

Printed and bound in the United Kingdom

ISBN 978-1-84078-625-5

Contents

7   CSS: Giving your pages some style   107

1 The web design challenge

Web design is the art of creating websites that are attractive and easy to use. But it's complicated by all the different browsers and devices visitors use. Learn about the principles for building a site that keeps everyone happy.

Hot tip

You can find supporting resources for this book, including all the links from it (so you don't have to type them in) at www.ineasysteps.com or www.sean.co.uk

The goal of this book

The most exciting thing about the Internet is not the way it's transformed virtually every industry, nor the way it's enabled us all to be better informed about the world, and more in touch with our family and friends, than ever before.

It's the fact that anyone can join in. If you've got something to share, the world is waiting.

You don't need anyone's permission to set up a website. You don't even need that much money: you can sometimes host a site for free and can rent a domain name for a year for about $10 or £10. Of course, you might choose to invest a bit more. You might want to pay for professional hosting with more advanced features.

If you're promoting your business, you might prefer to commission professional designers, and maybe even pay someone to help promote your site.

If you're doing it all yourself, you'll most likely pay through the time you spend on the design, although you might splash out on some software that makes it easier.

In this book, I'll teach you the key principles of web design, which is the art and science of building effective and attractive websites. This book will introduce you to the key technologies of the web, and the design principles that underpin successful sites.

Whether you're a budding designer who plans to build your own site, or you just want to be able to talk to professional designers in their own language, this book will give you an understanding of how websites are designed, so that you can make the right decisions in launching your own site.

I won't lie to you and tell you that website design can be mastered in 240 pages. The best websites are built using a combination of technical and artistic skill, and a good understanding of how people use the Internet. Above all, it takes practice to learn how to make the most of the technologies the web offers.

But, as the philosopher said, every journey begins with a single step. And this book will ensure you set off in the right direction, with robust knowledge of not just the technologies and techniques you could use, but of those that you should use, and those that will deliver the best experience for your visitors.

The diversity of devices

One of the skills a web designer needs is the ability to put themselves into the shoes of the website visitor. Web designers have to think about what their visitors know, what they will expect the website to do, and how they will expect it to work.

The most basic part of this is understanding the range of different devices that people might use to view your website. These include:

- A desktop computer, laptop or netbook

- An Android phone, iPhone or other handheld device

- A tablet device, such as an iPad

- An cell phone with a small screen and keypad

- A screenreader, which reads web pages aloud to blind people

- A refreshable Braille display, which a blind person can run their fingers along to read the website content

- A games console, such as the PlayStation, Nintendo Wii or Nintendo 3DS

When we use the word "design", we tend to think of something visual. But, in its purest sense, a website isn't necessarily a visual medium. Somebody using a screenreader might experience it as a stream of spoken text. Some handheld devices with small screens include a mode to switch off the layout and just view the content, so that it fits better in the space available.

While you do need your website to look appealing, it's a mistake to think that you can (or should) focus purely on the look of a website. Some of the most important work in web design goes on behind the scenes, where the visitors can't see it. It's about adding meaning to the web page, so that people can use it easily even if their device doesn't support all the features available on a desktop computer.

The challenge of web design is to create a site that is engaging and easy to use, whatever is used to view it. Visitors want the flexibility to use whichever device they prefer. Sometimes they will combine devices, using a desktop during their lunch break at work and a mobile on the way home, for example. All they care about is whether the site works or not. It's your job to make sure it does.

Websites can be viewed using a number of different devices. Shown above, from the top: Apple iPad tablet; Nintendo DS games console; HTC mobile phone; Alva refreshable Braille display.

How devices affect design

Different devices have different capabilities, and this should inform the decisions you make while designing your website. For example:

Web browsers are mostly free of charge, so why not download a few of the popular ones so that you can try them out? You'll get a taste of how they differ from your browser of choice, and can use them for testing your website design as it evolves.

12

- There might be no support for pictures (or "graphics") on the device. A screenreader and Braille display can't show images, and mobile devices sometimes enable users to switch them off to speed up their browsing.

- There might be no conventional keyboard. It puts everyone off if they have to type in lots of information to use a website, but those who have to use a virtual keyboard on their touchscreen might be especially deterred.

- The website animation technology Flash might not be supported. The iPhone and iPad don't use Flash, and non-visual devices (such as screenreaders) can't render it either.

- There might be no mouse. Some users struggle to use a mouse because of physical impairment, and some devices (including games consoles and netbooks) don't have a mouse. If you demand precise use of a mouse, you might lose visitors.

- There is a wide range of screen sizes. Even on a desktop computer, people will have different sized monitors and will open the browser window to different widths, depending on what else they're doing at the same time as web browsing. Designers tend to have large monitors, but they shouldn't forget that most of their audience have to settle for smaller screens.

- Devices differ in how much of the web page can be seen at once. Mobile devices might provide a small picture of the whole web page with little detail, so users can identify the content to zoom in on. Clear headings are important to help users navigate to the section they should read. Users with poor vision sometimes use screen magnifiers to massively enlarge a small part of the screen. If people are zoomed in on one part of the page, they can't see any updates you make to a different part of it.

- A screenreader user can't get a quick overview of what's on the page by skim-reading it: while a PC screen is two-dimensional, a screenreader has a one dimensional interface: a stream of audio reading the web page aloud.

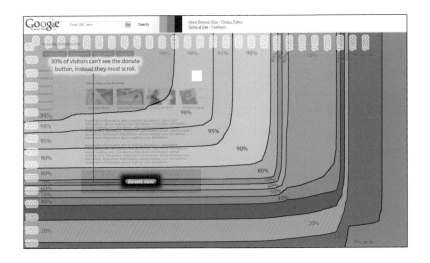

Left: Google mocked up a charity website to show that 30% of people can't see the donation button without scrolling if it's too far down. In Google Analytics (see Chapter 16), you can see a similar graph for your website. Go to the Behaviour section on the left, then click In-Page Analytics, and click the Browser Size button on the right.

The web browser challenge

As well as the differences in hardware used to visit websites, people often have a choice over which software they use. On a desktop computer, they might be using Microsoft's Internet Explorer or Apple's Safari browser. They might have downloaded Google's Chrome browser or the Firefox browser.

They might even use more than one browser, depending on whether they're at work or at home.

That's another reason website design is a challenge: Web designers have to build sites that work with a wide range of different browsers, and each browser has its own quirks.

It doesn't end there, though. These browsers are updated regularly, but not everybody upgrades at the same time. Internet Explorer version 8 (IE8) was released in 2009, but it is the last version to work on Windows XP, so it's likely to have a significant market share for some time yet.

Despite high profile campaigns in the web community to persuade people to switch to something more secure and more fully featured, many people are still using IE6, which was released way back in 2001. If you're a web designer, you can choose to ignore it, but are you willing to turn away those customers? It's better to create a site that works for everyone, and let your visitors decide how they want to experience it.

Hot tip

Use your web analytics software to identify the most popular browsers among people who visit your website. Bear in mind, though, that anyone who can't use your website easily might just leave. See Chapter 16 for more on analytics.

13

Your website will also include a file for each image, and might also include files for audio recordings, videos and downloadable files like brochures in the printer-friendly PDF format.

How quickly a web page downloads depends on how many files it has, and how large they are in total. Each additional file results in another request to the server, which takes time, in addition to the time taken to download. To speed up a page, minimize the number of different image, style sheet, JavaScript and Flash files you use. You can minify your HTML, CSS and JavaScript, which means taking all the unnecessary spacing out to make files smaller. Major corporate sites set a limit of 300kb per page.

Introducing key technologies

A website is made up of lots of different technologies and types of file. Part of the challenge of web design is learning how to use these different tools and technologies together, and how to pick the right ones for each aspect of your design. We'll cover the most important of these later in the book, but for now, here's a summary of the role they can play in your website:

HTML

HTML is the main language used for writing web pages. When somebody downloads one of your web pages, the first thing they are sent is an HTML file. HTML enables you to describe the structure of your text content, and to tell the web browser where it can find the other files for the web page, including its images and CSS files. HTML5 is the latest version, but many people are still using browsers that don't support its new features, so you need to make sure that your website also works without these.

CSS

CSS is used for the design and layout of your web page. It contains instructions for colors, fonts, and the position of different elements on the screen. CSS3 is the latest version and introduces features like rounded corners and multiple background images.

JavaScript

JavaScript enables you to update your web page after it has downloaded, and to respond to user actions on it. Some people have written sophisticated games using JavaScript, but it's typically used for simple effects like refreshing the screen with the latest news, or revealing some new content on the page when somebody clicks on a tab. JavaScript is also often used to check that a form has been completed correctly (for example, by checking there is an @ sign in an email address). This check can be performed before the user submits the form, so that the user gets instant feedback. Not all devices support JavaScript, so you need to ensure that your site (especially its navigation) also works without it.

Java

Confusingly, Java and JavaScript are not the same thing at all. Java enables you to run little programs inside your web page, as long as the browser has a Java plug-in. It's extremely slow, so almost nobody uses it for new websites today. If you already have web content in Java, consider recreating it using JavaScript or Flash.

Flash

Adobe's Flash is used for more sophisticated interactions. You can use it to create animations and games or to display rich media, such as audio or video. Flash requires a plug-in to enable users to see and interact with its content. iPhone and iPad owners can't use Flash on their devices.

Like JavaScript, you shouldn't depend on Flash for features of your website you can easily implement another way.

AJAX

AJAX is a special way of using JavaScript to update a web page, by getting new information from the server without updating the whole web page. When you use Google Maps, for example, it doesn't download the entire planet's worth of maps to your computer. It just downloads the bits you want to see. If you zoom in, it downloads a higher resolution map of the area you're looking at. If you pan to another town, it fetches its map from the server. AJAX is the term used for the combination of technologies that enables the website to fetch the new information you need, whenever you need it. If you need to use AJAX techniques, you'll need to master HTML, CSS and JavaScript first.

Server scripting languages (PHP/MySQL)

There are a number of different server scripting languages, and they tend to go through fashionable phases. The most popular one today is PHP, but others include ASP and Perl. These enable you to write programs that run on the server, so that web pages can be customized for each visitor. This is particularly useful if the site needs to offer personalized content, such as a social networking site that will want to serve a different home page to each person depending on who their friends are.

Server side scripting languages are also used for sites with lots of pages. Their content can be stored in a database, and when somebody wants to look at it, the program on the server makes the web page HTML and sends it out. It saves you having to maintain hundreds of web pages, because you can just take care of one template, the scripting program, and the database of content. See Chapter 13 for more on content management systems, which enable you to do this.

A plug-in is software that is added to a browser to enable it to handle new types of content. If users don't have the plug-in, they won't be able to view that content, so you'll need to provide alternative content, too. Very few websites will be able to convince people to install software just to view that site, so you should stick to using plug-ins that are already popular.

MySQL is the name of the database software most often used with PHP. Hosting companies will charge a bit more for servers that support PHP and MySQL, but can usually help you to set up the database. You can find lots of free PHP scripts you can install on your server to offer features like forums.

Degrading gracefully

You might be thinking that the solution is to create a different website for all the different user groups you have. You're not the first to think of this.

Some years ago, it was fashionable for organizations to create a separate, text-only version of their website for the benefit of screenreader users. These users have requirements that are extremely different to the typical PC user, so many companies thought it would be easier to make a separate site for them than to reconcile their needs with those of mainstream website visitors.

Having a separate screenreader site created two major problems. The first was that this site inevitably ended up getting neglected. When resources were scarce, website managers would prioritize updating the main site. The text-only version would be put to one side and, ultimately, be forgotten. A screenreader user might visit the site for the latest news and find that it wasn't available to them, although it was available to others using the main website. The organization's attempt to look after blind visitors by specifically catering for their needs ultimately resulted in them being discriminated against.

The second problem was more subtle. Some screenreader users felt they were missing out because the organization had stripped out all the visual content. The fact that they couldn't see the content didn't mean that they weren't interested in what was in it, or what its message was. Pictures often provide context or supporting information for text or visitor comments.

One site for all

Today, it's not necessary to create a separate website for specific audiences. There are too many different devices and configurations for you to cater for them all anyway. Instead, you should aim to create a single website design that degrades gracefully. That means that it can still be used if particular features aren't available on the visitor's device or browser. For example, if somebody can't see a photo, you should provide text that explains its content. If the web browser doesn't support content created using Flash or Javascript, visitors should still be able to navigate the site and use the rest of its content.

A well designed website will work on any device and web browser.

Take every opportunity to try out your website on unfamiliar devices. It's impractical for most people to own every device available, but if you come across one in a shop or at a friend's house, don't miss the chance to see how your site performs.

A website could use the new CSS3 properties to create rounded corners on a box of content. If the browser doesn't support CSS3, the box will have square corners instead. This is a good example of degrading gracefully. The content can all still be accessed, but its presentation has adapted to work on a more limited browser.

What about mobile?

There is one exception to the rule of "one site for all", which you might have come across. Many companies today are creating separate mobile websites. The difference in size between the largest available PC screen and the smallest mobile screen is so vast, some companies argue that serving two separate websites is the best way to keep both audiences happy.

While websites should always be optimized for speed, users of mobile devices often have a slower web connection than those using a desktop PC, too, so they need a site that is optimized to download in small chunks, with excessive decorative images stripped out.

There are two times when it's a good idea to create a separate site for users of mobile devices, assuming a significant chunk of your audience might want to use mobile devices:

● **If you have a tiny website.** You can probably maintain two different versions of a website easily if it's only got five pages.

● **If you have a vast website.** If your site has hundreds of pages, you'll probably need to use a content management system for it (see Chapter 13). This should make it possible to have your mobile site automatically generated from the same database of articles as your main website. That will ensure your mobile site always reflects the same content as the main site, and will update at the same time.

It adds a lot of complexity to maintain more than one website, however you do it. You'll have to decide whether the extra work is justified for your website.

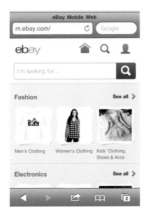 

Hot tip

Mobile sites like **m.ebay. com** and **mobile. wikipedia.org** streamline the site design so they're easy to read on mobile devices. Both sites use a single column, instead of the multiple column layout used on the main websites.

Understanding accessibility

Accessibility is all about making sure your website can be used easily by everybody. When people talk about accessibility, they often think of blind people using screenreaders. But it's not just about those who use completely different technologies to visit your website.

There are lots of people who have more subtle needs that you can help or hinder through the way you design your website. A lot of these people wouldn't consider themselves to have any special needs at all. They'd just find your website hard to use, and give up. For example:

- Can somebody who is color-blind understand the availability of tickets, or is it shown as purely different colored blobs?

- Can somebody who has impaired vision increase the font on your web page so it's easier to read?

- If somebody can't use the mouse, can they navigate your site using the keyboard?

- Can a visitor with impaired hearing get the same information that you've included in an audio file?

- Can somebody with a mental impairment understand your content, or is it too jargony and long-winded?

Most professional website designers today understand the importance of accessibility, but it's the least visible aspect of a website design project, so it can be overlooked. Much of the important work is to do with how a website is coded, and when you visit it using a conventional desktop PC, you can't easily tell whether it's been well designed for other devices or not.

Accessible websites tend to be easier for everybody to use. They adapt well to mobile devices, and are easier for search engines to index, too. If you need to convince colleagues of the importance of accessibility, you could argue that you want to reach as many customers as possible, or could point out that your business might contravene disability discrimination laws if you don't.

Most websites strive for accessibility because they want to be as inclusive as possible, though. It's not hard to make most websites accessible, and it doesn't cost any more, as long as you plan to make your site accessible from the start.

Hot tip

If you outsource your design, take particular care to make sure the designers are creating an accessible design. If you're never asked to provide any alternative text, ask yourself whether they're making it up for you, or not bothering with it at all.

Hot tip

Try navigating the web by keyboard for yourself, especially your own site when it's ready for testing. In Google Chrome, click a web page and then use the Tab key to move through the links. Press Enter to visit a link, and the Backspace key to go back a page. Use the Up and Down arrow keys to scroll the page.

Top accessibility principles

I'll share some tips for making your site accessible when we look at HTML and navigation later, but to provide some context, there are some basic principles that can go a long way towards making your site easy to use.

1. Provide alternative text for anything that isn't text, such as an image or video. This does not necessarily appear on screen. When you add an image to a web page, for example, you also provide alternative text that is only presented to the user if the image isn't available.

2. Make sure that your site still works when JavaScript, Flash or other interactive elements are switched off. When this is impossible, provide the same information in text form on an accessible web page.

3. If users have to respond within a certain time limit, make sure that they are warned and have enough time to request more time, if they need it. Give users controls to start and stop content that moves or updates itself.

4. Use clear and consistent navigation. Make sure that users can easily understand where each link will take them, and give each page a title that describes its purpose.

5. Make sure the website can be used with the keyboard, and that users can see what link or element they are focused on.

6. Make it easy to skip straight to the content. If your web page has a long list of links or header information, provide a link that enables people to jump straight to where the article starts. This is particularly important for screenreader users.

7. Don't open pop-up windows, or change the window the user is in, without warning. This is confusing if you can't see the screen, and it stops the Back button working, the most important navigational tool on the Internet.

Make sure your alternative text conveys the same information that it is replacing, but keep it brief. You can say "close up of clock tower", or "the gold detailing of Big Ben shines on a sunny day". Ask yourself what the purpose of the image is, and try to articulate that. You don't have to mention the blue skies, or where the big hand is pointing, unless it's important.

Hot tip

Don't provide alternative text for purely decorative images. Make these background images, so that assistive technology can ignore them.

...cont'd

Hot tip

For detailed guidance, see the Web Content Accessibility Guidelines (WCAG) published by web standards body W3C (**www.w3.org/ TR/WCAG20/**). Section 508 (**www.section508. gov**) outlines accessibility requirements for US government agencies, and includes good advice for all websites.

Hot tip

There are several automated accessibility checkers online, including Wave (**http:// wave.webaim.org/**) and Cynthia Says (**www. cynthiasays.com**). They test your website against the WCAG guidelines. They help to identify problems, but accessibility is about whether people can use your site, not whether it appears to tick a particular box. Use your own judgement and feedback from users, too.

8 Use the simplest language appropriate for your site's subject matter. Complicated language is harder to understand, especially if you can't easily flick your eyes back to the previous line for a refresher on what it said.

9 Give users control over how they view your content. Make sure your site works, for example, if people enlarge the default text size in their browser.

10 Make sure that any information conveyed by color can also be understood in other ways. For example, it's okay to use different colors to draw attention to different icons, but you might also make them different shapes or put them in different columns to indicate their meaning.

11 Make sure there is enough contrast in the foreground and background colors you choose for everything to be legible on a black and white screen.

12 Avoid overcomplicated page layouts. If there are too many different sections or boxes it can be overwhelming for visitors to try to navigate.

13 Use HTML and CSS correctly. Test whether the code has any errors in it. Desktop browsers can be quite forgiving, but assistive technology might struggle to understand your web page if it includes technical errors.

14 Use the accessibility features available in HTML to help people navigate tables and forms. They enable you to provide a context that might otherwise be communicated by the position of things on the screen.

15 Don't use a picture of text unless it's essential. It's a good way to show a company logo, for example. But don't create an image for a paragraph of text just because you like a particular font.

DIY or outsource?

Should you design your site yourself, or pay somebody else to do it for you? It depends on what you want to achieve with your website design project.

The strengths of DIY

Creating your own website can be an extremely satisfying creative project. People build websites for the same reason they write novels and sing songs: it's fun, and it's rewarding to increase your expertise over time. Building websites has an added dimension, because what you make can be easily found by others, so you can get feedback. It's also a cost-effective approach, compared to hiring a team of professionals.

If you want to build your own website, you can take one of two paths. Firstly, you can learn how HTML and CSS work and code your site by hand. These technologies aren't too hard to learn, and this book includes a quick tour around their most important features to get you started. Hand coding your site gives you maximum control and flexibility.

Alternatively, you could use a visual design package. These enable you to build a website in the same way you might make a newsletter in a word processor. They make it much easier to get started with website design, although it can take a lot of effort to build something impressive.

Once you know how to create websites, you could buy a template and adapt it to accelerate your web design process.

Outsourcing your design

Working with a web design firm is likely to lead to more professional-looking results first time. You can benefit from the firm's experience of designing perhaps hundreds of websites. You can focus on your content and the site's purpose and don't have to worry too much about technical details.

That said, it's still *your* website, and you need to take responsibility for managing the designers. You need to understand enough about web design to know whether their proposals are a good idea or not, and what the technical limitations might be on any designs they propose.

You might also want to learn enough HTML and CSS to be able to edit the design after the project has ended.

If you commission somebody else to build your website, make sure you have the ability to update it easily later.

Make sure you plan enough time for designers to do a good job on your website. Design is a process, with designers suggesting ideas and you providing feedback, until you reach the design you want.

How to set up your website

Now that you understand the design challenge, you're ready to take it on! Here is an outline of the process, although your own project might include extra steps, such as getting the CEO to approve the content:

1. **Planning.** Time invested in planning at the start will avoid rework later. In particular, a clear understanding of the site's purpose should inform the whole process.

2. **Content creation.** You need to write your text and gather your pictures so that the website can be designed to present them in the best way.

3. **Web design.** This involves many small steps. You'll need to structure your content, and design how it is presented. You also need to think about how people will move between different parts of your website. You might want to integrate a shopping cart or social networking features. You can commission a web design firm, or you can learn the technologies to design it yourself.

4. **Testing.** To make sure your design works, you need to test it at regular intervals. Design is often an experimental process, with the designer implementing an idea, testing it with prospective site visitors, and using the feedback to refine the design.

5. **Launching the website.** To make your website available to the public, you need to copy it onto a web server, which will send the web pages to your site visitors over the Internet. You will need to rent web server space from a hosting company.

6. **Promoting the website.** Attract visitors by making it easy for people to find your site through search engines, adverts, and links.

7. **Measuring your success.** Find out how well your site is fulfilling its purpose, and use that information to refine it.

2 Planning your website

Before you design your site, you need to think about its goals, competition, and audience; about how you will organize its content; and how visitors will interact with it. You should also research web design firms, if you want to use one.

The purpose of your website

It might be tempting to dive straight in and start designing your website, but, before you do anything, you need to stop and think. Why are you building a website in the first place? What do you want it to achieve?

The answers to those questions will have an impact on the way you design the site, the features you build into it, and the content you use. In fact, they should have an influence on every part of the project. Everything you do will either be working towards or away from those goals.

Think of the benefits your new website will bring to you, and to your visitors. Here are some of the things that a website could help you to do:

- **Build new relationships.** Whether you're looking for customers, investors, fans for your band, or just want to connect with peers who share your interests, then having a website can help you attract them from all over the world.

- **Enhance your reputation and profile.** If you want to be known as an expert, then sharing articles or videos that demonstrate your expertise can help. If you're creative, then sharing your music, photos, videos or stories can help you to solicit feedback and build interest in your ideas.

- **Sell, sell, sell!** Of course, you can use the web to make it easier for people from all over the world to buy from you. For digital content, such as music, you can even make it possible for the product to be delivered without human intervention.

- **Improve customer service.** If you have an existing business, you might be able to make it easier for customers to deal with you by publishing manuals and tutorials online. You could take customer enquiries, too, and structure the form so that you capture all the information needed to resolve the query first time. Using the web, any business, no matter how small, can offer some degree of customer service round the clock.

- **Educate.** Whether you want to help the market understand your latest invention, or just want to help others learn a hobby, tutorials are amongst the most sought-after content on the web.

- **Entertain.** Internet users love fun sites, and the web is the ideal medium for sharing short games, films and songs.

- **Create a community.** People like to socialize with and seek advice from others who share their interests online, and many successful websites exist primarily to bring people together. Many of the biggest websites today (including Facebook, Twitter, and Flickr) have been built on the idea of community and of creating new ways for people to communicate.

- **Create new services.** The lines between the website, the product, and the manufacturing process are often blurred. Vistaprint (**www.vistaprint.com**), for example, enables people to design their own business cards, calendars and T-shirts online, which are then professionally printed and delivered by mail. Some websites charge readers a subscription, so the website content is itself the product.

- **Make money.** You might make money by placing advertising against your website content, selling products, or cutting your costs if you already have a conventional business. This can be a strong motivator to build a website, but take care that you don't undermine the end user's experience. You might make more money by plastering adverts everywhere, but you won't win the loyalty of visitors.

There are lots of other things a website could help you with, and you might well find that you want to do more than one of the above. The important thing is that you understand why you're building a site. Otherwise, you might get to the end of your design project and find your site doesn't help you at all.

The web can be a relatively cheap way to test new product ideas, and to communicate with customers, so you can often afford to be a bit more experimental online than you might be in an offline business.

Google's Adsense (**www. google.com/adsense**) enables you to host adverts on your website and get paid. Your income will depend on how many people click on the adverts, which will, in turn, depend on how many people visit your site.

Left: Vistaprint enables you to customize calendars, business cards and T-shirts online.

Don't forget

Your competition online might be very different to your real-world competition, if you have a business. For example, you might be competing with independent review sites and amateur blogs online. People researching the products you sell might well end up at these sites instead of your online shop.

Hot tip

You can learn a lot by spending time on your competitors' sites, too. Study the language and design they use to communicate with their audience, and if they have a public forum, check the customer feedback there.

Right: Alexa offers market intelligence on websites, including traffic levels and search engine keywords that delivered visitors.

How will you compete?

With a website, the competition is only one click away. When people see your site in search engine listings, they'll see your direct competitors at the same time. When they see a link to your site, it will almost certainly be among many other links. If you advertise your site on another site, you need to compete for attention with the content people choose to see in the first place. What do you offer that's special enough to entice visitors to your site?

Companies often talk about having a "unique selling proposition" (or USP), which is a fancy way of saying what differentiates them from the competition. You need to think in terms of how your website benefits the visitor. What do you do better than all the hundreds of similar sites out there? It's easier to compete if you can, in some way, be unique.

It pays to do some basic market research early on. Find out which other sites cater for your audience, what they do well, and where you can make improvements. To find potential rivals, think broadly. Search the web for names of products, people, places, and benefits. For example, if you're building a site for a book shop, search for the names of authors and books, the subject area of a book you sell (such as "learn web design"), your town, plus the phrase "book shop" (and "bookshop" too).

When you find a site of interest, Alexa (**www.alexa.com**) can provide detailed intelligence, including estimated traffic levels, visitor demographics, reviews, related links, and popular keywords that deliver traffic there from search engines.

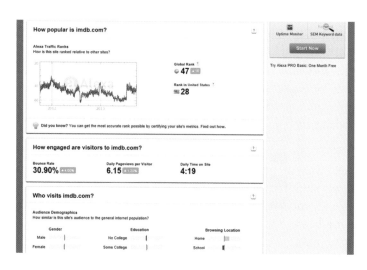

Understanding your visitors

As well as researching the competition, it's important to have a good understanding of who your website visitors, or customers, will be. You can't create a site that pleases everyone, so you need to focus on the preferences of those who you most want to reach.

Try to understand, for example:

- Are they predominantly male or female, or are they likely to be a reasonably even mixture?

- What stage of life are they at? Are they children, or are they grown up with children of their own? Do they study or work? Are they senior citizens? The kind of design that appeals will vary greatly by age and background.

- How much disposable income could they spend with you? How sensitive are they to pricing?

- What are they interested in outside of your website? Can you use any ideas from popular culture or literature that might appeal to them?

- How experienced are they at using the Internet? Beginners will need more reassurance to make the most of your site, but experts will be happy to experiment and fearless about making mistakes.

- Where do they use the Internet? Do they pay by the minute in an Internet cafe, do they sneak a quick surf at work, or do they view your site at leisure at home?

- What kind of device will they use to view your site? The latest trendy mobile device, or a beaten-up old computer?

27

Hot tip

Once your site is up and running, you can learn a lot about visitors by studying your web analytics. For now, think about your ideal visitors, and research the visitors of competitive sites.

Different designs for different audiences.

Top: a company selling information to financial services companies (www.timetric.com) has a business-like layout and a focus on textual information.

Bottom: The communication design department at Kutztown University of Pennsylvania (www.kutztown.edu/acad/commdes) has a website with an emphasis on graphic design, which will appeal to its students.

Creating a sitemap

One of the challenges of creating your website is to organize your content into meaningful sections. What those sections are will depend on the content of your site, and its purpose, but you could carve your site up into:

- Product types, brand names, or product names

- Audiences, such as buyers and sellers

- Areas of interest, such as environmental news, technology news and book reviews

- Classes of content, such as stories, games, and videos

- Activities that site visitors can undertake, such as shopping, reviewing or downloading

The important thing is that the grouping makes sense to your prospective visitors. It should be possible for visitors to find what they need without having to click between all the different sections to hunt for it. If somebody was reading a page about a camera you sell, they wouldn't expect to have to go to two different sections to read reviews on it and see videos about it. In that case, it would make more sense to organize all that content in a single section dedicated to that camera.

If your content is diverse, or you have a large catalogue of products, you can use subcategories, too. You could have a top category of cameras, with subcategories for consumer cameras, semi-professional cameras and professional cameras. Or you might have a main category for cameras, which contains subcategories for different brands.

Think like a customer

It's easy to forget that customers don't use the jargon you do, and might not be familiar with your site's content. A lot of businesses create sites that closely mirror how their company divisions are organized, but that often makes no sense at all to outsiders. Visitors don't know where to start looking for what they need.

Try to use simple language to define each section. If you can't do that, then consider reorganizing the sections, or creating subcategories to reduce complexity.

Hot tip

You can create a page on your website that has links to all the pages on it, and this is often called a sitemap, too. It can help people if they get lost or can't find something on your site. Search engines can also use it to discover all your website's content.

28

As well as defining how the content is split up, you need to have a sense of how the sections are related to each other: what content deserves to be on the homepage, for example, and what content can be pushed a few clicks away from it.

Developers often create a sitemap, which represents the way the site sections are linked to each other, similar to the way that a roadmap might represent connected neighborhoods.

It doesn't really matter how you make this. One approach is to write the section names on to sticky notes, and then arrange them into a sequence that makes sense, drawing lines between them to represent connections and hierarchy. You can easily add, remove and reposition sections by moving the sticky notes around.

Below you can see two different sitemaps for a band website, mostly based on the same content, but placing a different emphasis. The first, for example, has the shop as a major section. The second pushes free music to the homepage and sells through the music section.

Hot tip

The sitemap doesn't need to include every link on your site, nor every piece of content. It's just an overview of the main paths people can take to get between the main content areas. Don't feel you have to represent every single page.

29

Asking your customers to help

To help you work out the categories that products belong to, you can ask some of your customers or target audience to carry out a card sorting exercise. To do that, you give them a set of cards with the names of the different content areas or pages on them. They then organize them into groups that make sense to them, suggesting some category names too. You could also ask them how they think the categories should relate to each other. Make sure you use a representative sample of potential customers if you carry out this exercise. Don't rely too much on one person's view.

Planning interaction

Something that has a huge impact on a site's development is the degree of interactivity it enables. Every site allows people to navigate it using links, of course, and most enable the use of contact forms and search boxes.

Some websites, though, enable much more sophisticated interactions and become almost indistinguishable from software. Facebook is as fully featured as any email program, for example. Adobe has online photo editing software, including Adobe Photoshop Express Editor (**www.photoshop.com/tools**):

Hot tip

Don't overcomplicate your site. If all you want to do is publish information, it's okay to have a simple website with basic interaction.

Think about how you want people to interact with your content. For example, do you want them to be able to vote or comment on their favorite pages? Do you want to include an interactive tutorial that explains how your technology works? What about enabling people to customize content and download it, like the photo editing example above? Do you want people to be able to connect with their friends and share information with them?

In short: what kind of experience do you want your website visitor to have? And what will you empower them to do?

Hot tip

Later in this book, you'll learn how to hide and reveal parts of the web page in response to user requests, how to accept comments, and how to make simple Flash animations.

In many web design projects, the degree and type of interaction determines the complexity and cost. Flash animation requires more specialist design skills, for example, and any website that involves storing data from visitors will need software to be installed on the server. In many cases, that software will need to be written especially for the website, which can be expensive.

Hosting your website

Your website is made up of files that are stored on a computer that people can access over the Internet. This computer is known as a web server. These files will include the text, graphics and layout instructions for your website, among other things.

When somebody wants to see one of your web pages, their browser will request it over the Internet. The server will send them back the files they need for that web page, and the browser will combine them all and present them to the user.

Few people who run a website ever see their server. They work with a hosting company, which rents them a server, or, more usually, just some space on a shared server. These servers are kept in data centers with high availability and dedicated technical teams to respond to any faults.

When you have a shared server, the monthly costs will be tiered according to two parameters:

- **Storage space.** This is how much space all your website files occupy on disk. If you will allow users to contribute content that is stored on your server, then you need to count this, too.

- **Bandwidth.** This is how much data you can send over the Internet each month. This is a function of how many visitors you have, how many pages they look at, and how big the files are on your website.

Usually, you can start small and upgrade as the scope and popularity of your site grows. Sometimes, you will need to start with a more expensive account, because you want to use technologies that have special hosting requirements, such as PHP, and these cost more. It's worth researching hosting early, so that you can launch as soon as your site is ready.

It can be hard to find a good hosting company online, because there are so many intermediaries vying to make money by promoting hosting companies. Sometimes these companies are basically reselling the hosting service, so their business isn't hosting at all. It's marketing. The best place to find a hosting company is through adverts in computer or Internet magazines.

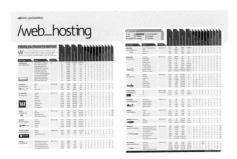

/web_hosting

Left: .net magazine publishes a summary table of hosting companies each month

Well established hosting companies include GoDaddy.com, 1&1 (**www.1and1.com**) and Fasthosts (**www. fasthosts.co.uk**). If you work with a web design company, they will usually take care of the hosting for you.

To work out whether you own your domain name, ask yourself whether you own the bit immediately before the domain extension. For example, I don't own sean.example.com, because I don't own example.com

Once you have your hosting and domain name, you can publish a simple holding page to tell people what you will launch there and when. Include some search engine keywords (see Chapter 15) so search engines can start building a profile of your domain.

Why domain names matter

Each web page on the Internet has a unique address, which is known as its URL (short for Uniform Resource Locator). For example: **www.nytimes.com/pages/world/index.html**

This URL is broken down into several different parts:

- **The domain name:** This is the address of the website, and is used to find the server that hosts the files. All the files on the same website will start with the same domain name. In this example, the domain name is nytimes.com. The .com part is the domain extension, and it describes what kind of website this is (a commercial one).

- **The folders:** These explain where the required file is on the server. In our example, the folders are /pages/world/ and it means the file is inside the "world" folder, which is, itself, inside the "pages" folder. This is similar to the way that folders are sometimes described on a Windows PC.

- **The filename:** This is the specific web page, in this case, index.html, which is one of the traditional names for the start page in any particular section of the website. The .html at the end is the file extension and it explains that this is a HTML file. Image files will have a different extension, such as .jpg.

It is possible to launch a website without having your own domain name, but I wouldn't recommend it. Some years ago, lots of musicians built websites, which were all hosted by MP3.com and which all shared the MP3.com domain name. When that business was sold on, all those pages were shut. Bands lost the audience they had spent years building up, and all the incoming links they had. Fans lost contact with the bands because their bookmarks no longer worked. If your site is hosted on somebody else's domain name, then that organization has absolute control over your website.

Owning your domain name gives you independence. If your hosting company messes you around, you can go to a different hosting company instead, and take your domain name with you. Visitors can still find you, and all your incoming links will continue to work.

Domain names are cheap, often less than $10 or £10 a year, and are one of the best investments you can make in your website.

8 domain name buying tips

Here are some top tips for buying your domain name:

1 Any reputable hosting company can tell you whether a domain is already registered or not.

2 It's usually easier and cheaper to buy your domain name from your hosting company.

3 Keep it short. Your visitors will often have to type it in.

4 Make it memorable and avoid things that can't be spelled easily, or would need to be spelled out on the phone.

5 Your domain extension can help you tell visitors what kind of site you have. There are extensions for different countries, and types of sites, for example: .co.uk for UK companies, .me.uk for personal websites, .ca for Canadian websites, .mobi for mobile sites, .biz for businesses. You can use .com, .info, .net and .org for anything. You can invent creative domains using the extensions of foreign countries, such as .tv (Tuvalu) or .me (Montenegro).

6 Don't try to buy all the different variants of your domain name. You'll go both mad and broke. There are way too many. It might be worth buying a couple of domains for key markets you want to work in (such as the .com and .co.uk variants, if you intend to create different websites for the US and UK). But otherwise, it's best to accept that you can't own every variant.

7 Search engines will consider any keywords in your domain name to be important, but don't overdo it. You could have something like www.bloggs-bakery.com, but you wouldn't want to have www.bloggs-bakery-bread-boston.com. It makes you look desperate for visitors.

8 As soon as you work out the domain you want, buy it! Others might be interested in that same domain and if you snooze, you lose!

The US never really took to its regional extension of .us. Most US websites use .com

Take care not to register a domain name that includes a word or phrase that somebody else has trademarked in your market sector. You might lose the domain name if they object.

Whenever a new extension is announced, there's a rush to register domains. Preregistration with a registrar doesn't guarantee you'll get the domain. It just means your chosen registrar will join the race on your behalf, up against other registrars who might be after the same domains.

34

Make sure your domain isn't ambiguous. **www.goredfoxes.com** should be read "Go Red Foxes", the name of an athletics team, not "gored foxes", for example. There are many more hilarious (and rude) examples at **www.slurls. com**. Don't let your domain name join them!

Domain name pitfalls

Domain names are valuable assets, so it's important to look after yours. There are several scams involving domain names which you should be aware of, although they are thankfully becoming less common now than they used to be.

Firstly, the renewal date of your domain name is a matter of public record. Rival domain registration companies sometimes phone up or post letters that look like invoices and ask you to renew. While they consider this to be clever marketing, a lot of people think of it as a scam. Many people are tricked into transferring management of their domain name to another company, and, even if the site continues to be well hosted, do you want to deal with a company that markets itself like that?

To protect yourself from this scam, know when your domains are due for renewal, and beware of any communications that come too early or from organizations you haven't dealt with before. If you get any paperwork you don't understand, ask your current hosting company or web designers to explain it.

Another scam involves companies phoning you up to try to sell you domain names you don't need. They will often say they have another client who is about to register a domain name that is similar to your company name or existing domain name, but they want to give you first refusal. You can safely ignore this. If the domain name is registered and hosts a competitive website, laws that prevent others trading on your goodwill protect you. If the domain name is registered and used for an unrelated purpose, it's not doing you any harm. In most cases, it will never be registered, of course, because the client who was about to register the domain is entirely fictional.

You need to take care when you're researching your domain name, too. Some unscrupulous domain registrars will register domains you express an interest in but do not immediately register, in the hope that they can sell them to you at an inflated price later. Only check the availability of your domain name on a reputable hosting company's website. You can also check who owns a website (if anyone) by running a "whois" search at the Internet registry for an extension, which is basically the organization in charge of it. For .com domains, see **http://www.internic.net/whois.html** For .co.uk domains, see **www.nominet.org.uk**

Working with web designers

You can design your website yourself, but many people prefer to work with professional web designers. They bring the experience gained from working on lots of previous projects, and the level of expertise that comes from developing websites full time.

If you decide to work with a web design firm, you still need to understand what makes a website effective, and need to make sure that your site meets your goals. Your designers will bring a lot of creativity and insight to your brief, but you will need to work with them to manage the project successfully.

Choosing a good designer

You can find web design firms through a search engine, through adverts in magazines, or through your local phone book. You can find freelancers worldwide, through Elance (**www.elance.com**). Designers often work remotely, without meeting their clients, but you might prefer to work with somebody local.

Take a look at the web designer's own website, as well as those in his or her portfolio. Don't be seduced by flashy graphics, unless they would help you to satisfy your site's purpose. Look at how easy the sites are to use, and how well they meet their objectives. Try resizing the web browser window, increasing the text size, navigating by keyboard, and typing nonsense into forms, to see if the site still works. See whether you can find the websites easily using a search engine, and try out the sites on different devices.

Often, the portfolio sites will have been designed with different requirements to your own, but you can learn a lot about a design firm by checking how flexible and search-engine friendly their sites are by default.

How web designers charge

Web designers usually quote a fixed fee for the project. This will be based on their estimate of how much time it will take them, considering the scope of your design project and how easy you will be to work with. If you can reassure them that you will respond promptly to their requests for feedback and input, and supply materials in a form that's ready to go on the website wherever possible, you might be able to save money. There can also be regular maintenance costs, and it's good idea to incentivize your designer to have an ongoing interest in the success of your website, if you think you might need their help to keep it running.

Some web design firms specialize in creating sites for particular market sectors. Try searching for something like "web design law firm" to see if there are any companies who specialize in your line of business.

Make sure you have a formal contract with your web designer, and that it transfers the copyright of the website design and related materials to you.

Hot tip

Ask designers what tools they will use. If they're using standard components (such as WordPress and jQuery) to build your site, it will be easier for someone else to maintain in the future, if necessary. If they're building everything from scratch for you, and the site has sophisticated interactive features, it will be much harder.

Hot tip

A good understanding of web design, gained from reading the rest of this book, will help you to understand and manage your design team.

...cont'd

When to engage your web designers

It can take some time to find designers you trust, so it's a good idea to start looking as soon as possible. However, you should probably wait until your content has been created before you kick off the design project. Otherwise you run the risk of having to cut your content to fit the design.

Finishing the content first also means you can then focus your attention on the design, which makes it easier for you to provide timely testing and feedback.

How to brief your designers

To get the best results from your web designers, give them the freedom to be creative. If you have a clear vision for your website, by all means share it. But don't dictate the layout, color scheme, navigation, and so on, unless you're certain you've got a better design than they might otherwise have come up with.

Instead, start by sharing those aspects of the site you have already planned. Tell them about the website purpose, and how you plan to differentiate your site from the competition. Provide as much information as you have on your audience and the kinds of devices they might use to view your website. Share your concept of how you want visitors to interact with your website, and send them the content you already have.

If you can provide examples of competitive (or even unrelated) websites that you love and hate, and explain why, that will help the designers gauge your taste.

Designers will often create mock-ups of the design, using an art package like Photoshop at first, so that you can agree on the look and feel of the site before they spend too much time developing web pages. When you have alternative designs to choose from, it's usually okay to mix and match ideas from them. These mock-ups are part of the web design project, and you shouldn't expect designers to speculatively create them for free.

Providing feedback

Keep in touch with your design team and provide timely and regular feedback. Make sure that you thoroughly proofread and test the final web pages. Ultimately, you are responsible for the quality of your own website.

3 Creating effective website content

Once you've planned your site, the next step is to think about its content. You could use text, photos, cartoons, audio, video, maps or games to get your message across.

Hot tip

Make the most of the content you already have. You might be able to reuse information from brochures, CVs or resumés, and conferences.

Beware

If you publish an email address online, it will attract junk mail. You could register a free email account and use that for web queries, to protect your main address. Alternatively, you could accept queries through a form, so that your email address isn't published. You can use a CAPTCHA on the form to stop automated submissions. This is a simple puzzle that requires human intelligence to solve, such as reading some distorted text.

Ideas for content

Before you can consider designing your website, you need to create your content. Doing it the other way around is a bit like designing the packaging before coming up with the product idea: it might work, but you'll probably have to chop a few bits off the product to fit it in the box.

The content you choose to publish will be determined by your site's purpose and the message you want to get across.

Essential content for every website

- **About us/me.** When visitors arrive at your site, they might not know anything about you. Some context about who you are, what you do, and why you're different, helps them understand everything else on your site.

- **Contact page.** Even if you're not selling, it's good to have a dialogue with your visitors. You'll be surprised how helpful some visitors can be, telling you about broken links and similar issues. If you are selling, it's essential to reassure customers that they can contact you with any problems.

Content ideas for business sites

- **How to find us.** Make it easy to find your office or shop.

- **Meet the team.** The web can seem impersonal, so put a friendly face on it by introducing your team members.

- **Product and service descriptions and photos.** People won't buy something they can't understand. Be clear about what you offer and why customers should buy from you.

- **Customer service information.** Answer the most frequently asked questions (FAQs) in advance. Customers get an instant answer, and you save the time spent answering personally. Product instructions can be particularly valuable.

- **Customer testimonials.** Ask your existing customers to share their success stories and reviews.

- **Behind the scenes.** Lift the lid on your business with a photo tour of the factory, or an overview of how you work.

- **Presentations.** Share audio, video and/or slides from any talks you deliver. Consider making tutorial videos purely for use on the website.

Content ideas for any website

- **Blog**. Have a regularly updated section where you comment on what's going on in your business, what's in the news, and what you're thinking. Blogs are expected to be opinionated and often encourage readers to leave their comments.

- **What's new.** Keep the website fresh with the latest news in your industry, company, or area of interest.

- **Tutorials.** People often turn to the web when they need help. Demonstrate your expertise and draw in new readers with articles that teach people how to fix things, make things, or do things.

- **Games.** Can you get your message across in a game? Games will make your site more memorable, and encourage longer visits. The British Heart Foundation created a Yoobot vs Yoonot game to teach healthy eating and exercise habits (**www.yoobot.co.uk**).

- **Calculators and tools:** Can you help people to solve a simple problem? You could incorporate a simple tool like a tax calculator, a picture resizer or dictionary. Ask yourself, what do your customers look for online that you can offer.

- **Interviews:** Can you interview an expert in your field and share their wisdom with your site visitors?

Hot tip

Consider using a mixture of different formats for your content. Text is ideal for attracting new visitors through search engines, short videos are popular with many people, and some will download a podcast to listen to during their commute.

39

Beware

All content is automatically protected by copyright. If you didn't create something, make sure you get permission from its creator before using it. Duplicate text can be penalized by search engines, so it pays to invest in creating your own.

Visitors will use the quality of your writing as an indicator of the quality of your expertise and/or service. It's difficult to proofread and edit your own work, so get a friend (or, ideally, a professional) to check your copy.

What about PDFs? These are files that preserve the look of a brochure, and which you can put on your site for download. If somebody arrives at a PDF file through a link or search engine, though, they won't see your navigation. Their only option is to leave your site again. It's better to adapt the content from the PDF and incorporate it into your web pages properly.

How web writing differs

Writing for the web is different to writing for printed documents for a few reasons:

- People skim-read web pages, so good use of subheadings and lists is essential for getting your message across.

- Search engines will deliver people to the page that most closely matches their query, not necessarily your homepage. People can start reading at any page on your site, so you can't assume they have read any other pages.

- Sometimes people arrive at your site after following a link they've seen elsewhere. Their expectations of your site will be defined by the text of that link, and any surrounding commentary. This is usually outside of your control.

- People can take any path through your content, following links to explore other sections at any time. You can provide links to background information, so you don't need to clog the story up with excessive detail.

To account for all this, make sure that people can easily work out where they are in your content. To a certain extent, this is a function of how the site and its navigation are designed, but you need to consider it in your content, too. You can't assume that people are reading every word from page one. If you do, you'll confuse visitors, and they'll abandon your site.

Use strong headlines and subheadings to help readers understand the purpose of each chunk of content, and how it relates to the rest of the page.

Don't try to railroad readers into following a linear path through your content. Use links to help people find related content that provides additional context. For example, don't tell people all sales are subject to shipping fees and then expect them to hunt for that information. Link it. If you mention other products, then add links to them too. If you give people different paths through your site, they're more likely to spend time exploring it.

You can put a link anywhere in a sentence, and readers will understand it's a path they could take, or they could ignore it. Make sure your link text is descriptive so that people know what they're likely to find if they click it.

8 top web writing tips

1. **Keep web pages reasonably short**. Focus on one topic on each page. It's easier to navigate a series of short pages that include clear links between them, than a rambling essay that fills five screenfuls.

2. **Put readers first.** Don't bang on about how great you are. Tell readers how they benefit, and make sure you are telling them what they want to know from the very first sentence. Reflect their interests in the headline.

3. **Use a strong headline.** Headlines with verbs (action words) are more compelling. Compare "Pink Floyd releases new album" with "New Pink Floyd album".

4. **Create a lively pace.** Start a new paragraph for each new idea, and keep paragraphs short. Vary the length of sentences but don't let any go on for too long.

5. **Be consistent.** Format dates and abbreviations consistently, and, where different spellings are possible, pick one and stick with it.

6. **Be specific.** Avoid hype like "award winning" and just say what you've won. Replace "affordable" with the price.

7. **Don't show off.** New writers feel that they have to put on a writerly voice, and end up driving away readers. Keep sentences simple, prefer shorter words, and avoid jargon. If you must use technical terms, define them as you go.

8. **Edit vigorously.** Make every word add meaning. Delete words like "actually", "indeed", "really", and "currently". Look out for phrases that have shorter alternatives. Replace "despite the fact that" with "although", for example. Avoid the passive voice: don't say "the mat was sat on by the cat"; do say "the cat sat on the mat".

Read it aloud. If you get out of breath mid-sentence, readers will have forgotten the start of the sentence when they get to the end. If you stumble over tricky phrases, readers will struggle to concentrate.

To help enforce consistency, refer to a journalism style guide. Reuters, The Economist, and The Guardian all publish theirs online for free.

How big do you need the picture to be? You can easily shrink digital pictures but can't enlarge them without losing quality, so start with the highest quality image you can find.

42

Hot tip

Make sure your photos look good. As a minimum, they need to be well exposed and in focus. Ideally, they should be well composed, too. Beware of people who have trees growing out of their heads, unsightly shadows and confusing composition.

Images that work

Web pages without any pictures look bland, but that's no excuse for covering your web page with decorative effects. The number and size of pictures on a website is often the biggest factor in determining how long it takes to download. So you need to be selective in those you use, and make sure they add maximum value for the visitor.

While it is okay to use some decorative images, the best pictures are those that inform or entertain, and that help you to tell your story. For example:

● Your logo, if you have one

● Pictures of the products you are selling or writing about

● Photos of your company's shops or offices, or places you are writing about

● Photos of yourself, the people on your team, or those you are writing about or interviewing

● Illustrations that help explain a tutorial, such as an assembly diagram for a computer

● Cartoon strips

● Artistic photos, if you built the site to share them

You will probably find that you already have lots of pictures you can put on your website. You can use photos taken with a digital camera, or can use a scanner to digitize old prints or negatives. You can usually get high quality product images from the product's manufacturer, too.

A scanner like this one from Canon can be used to scan both photos and negatives.

Left: Firebox (**www. firebox.com**) uses several different photos of its products, to give customers a complete view of how the product is used.

Smaller photos are used to illustrate similar products. When customers click these images, they're taken to the detailed product pages.

Firebox encourages customers to submit their own photos, too, by awarding a gift voucher to the best ones and the first ones of each product.

Your site will have more personality if you can create or commission your own images, rather than if you just use stock shots.

Pictures are protected by copyright. You can't just take a picture from somebody else's website without permission.

Photographers sometimes sell the same image through different libraries at different prices. You might be able to save money by shopping around.

Using stock photography

If you don't have images of your own, you could try licensing some from a stock photography library. Stock.xchng (**www. sxc.hu**) has a large catalogue of free photos. Paid libraries, like Dreamstime (**www.dreamstime.com**), Fotolia (**www.fotolia.com**) and iStockphoto (**www.istockphoto.com**), license images for different affordable prices, depending on how big a file you need. If you think you might want to use the photo in a brochure, too, it's worth buying the high quality version so you don't have to go back and buy another license later.

People occasionally upload photographs they don't own the copyright on, because they don't understand copyright. Exercise common sense, especially with photos of famous people or news events. Somebody can only give you permission to use a photo if it's theirs in the first place.

Just because something doesn't use a Creative Commons license, it doesn't necessarily mean you can't use it. Try searching for copyright-controlled images and ask the photographer if you may use any pictures you like.

Finding photos on Flickr

Flickr (**www.flickr.com**) is a photo sharing website. Some members make their photos available under a Creative Commons license, which means you can use their photos free of charge, without asking for permission.

There are still conditions attached: some photos cannot be used commercially, and you usually have to credit the photographer. Sometimes you can't modify the photo either. Here's how to find photos you can use on Flickr:

1 Go to the Flickr homepage (**www.flickr.com**) and enter your search keywords. Click the Search button. This will show you all images that match your keywords.

2 Click Advanced Search, underneath the Search box. Scroll down to the Creative Commons section and tick the box. Tick the boxes for photos allowing commercial use and adaptation, if necessary.

3 When you click Search, the results will be pictures you can use in your website. Click a photo to visit its page, where you can see the full license and leave your thanks for the photographer.

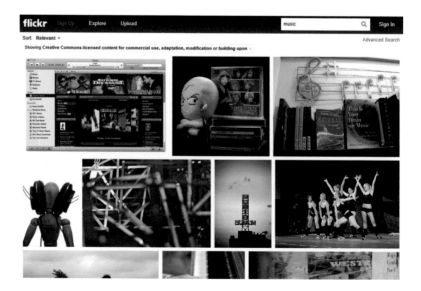

Creating a cartoon

You can find cartoonists online, and might find that a web design company is able to create a comic strip for you.

There are also lots of tools online that you can use to make your own comic. Pixton (**www.pixton.com**) is perhaps the most sophisticated. It charges a subscription fee to use its tools for making cartoons that you can use on your website.

Hot tip

If you see a cartoon you like online, you might be able to use that in your website. Some cartoonists provide HTML code you can use to embed the strip in your site. You just copy the HTML snippet and paste it onto your web page to add the cartoon. Other cartoonists might let you reuse their work, if you ask them.

There is a wide range of characters to choose from, and they are highly customizable. Using the editing tools, you can change the pose of the characters (including moving the limbs and rotating the body how you want); the color of skin, clothes and hair; and the shape of body parts. You can upload your own background images, so you could place characters in your own office, or you can use the illustrated backgrounds provided. You download the final cartoon as a JPG, PNG or PDF file.

Left: Google worked with cartoonist Scott McCloud (www.scottmccloud.com) to create a fantastic comic book explaining what was different about the Google Chrome browser. (www.google.com/googlebooks/chrome/)

Hot tip

Consider the size you will use the image at. Detailed pictures look muddy at smaller sizes. Large pictures can include more detail.

45

Compressing images

As well as the number of images you have, the file format you use for them has a big influence on your website's speed. There are three different image formats that are commonly used in websites, with most websites using a combination of at least two:

- **JPEGs:** This format is best for photographs. Depending on the level of compression you use, the image can lose some of its definition. You might see ghosting around the edges of objects, for example. Creating a good JPEG image involves striking a balance between the level of compression and how clear the image is onscreen.

- **GIFs:** A GIF image can have a maximum of 256 colors, so the format is best used for icons or other illustrations. The compression algorithm is lossless, which means you don't lose any image quality. You can also create animated GIFs, which combine a number of animation frames into a single image file. The browser displays the frames automatically, at your predefined intervals. GIF files can also have a transparent color, which allows the background to show through.

- **PNGs:** The PNG generally offers better compression than GIF and JPEG for icons and other computer art. It also supports more sophisticated transparency, with the ability to have transparent colors that let the background shine through. The adoption of PNG has been hampered by bugs or omissions in support from Internet Explorer (up to and including IE8), and there is no support in the format for animation.

Hot tip

Each time the page requests an image file, a script or a style sheet, it has to go back to the server, which causes a slight delay. CSS Sprites enable you to combine images into one file. They're beyond the scope of this book, but are worth researching if your design is heavily image-led.

46

Right: the PNG transparency enables the background to show through the colored dice.

Image created by Ed Sanders and contributed to the Wikimedia Commons.

...cont'd

To prepare your images for your website, follow these steps. You can use any image preparation program. If you don't have one, you can use the free Irfanview (**www.irfanview.com**).

1 You can tell the browser to display an image at any size on the screen and it will scale your picture up or down to fill the space. If you use a larger photo than you need, though, you'll slow your website unnecessarily. Photos from digital cameras and other high quality images will be much bigger than you need for a web page. Your first step, then, should be to resize the pictures so that they are the same size as you want to use them. For example, resize your photo from 4272 by 2848 pixels (width by height) so that it is 350 by 233 pixels. Take care to preserve the aspect ratio so your image is not distorted.

2 Save a copy of the image in your desired file format. For photos or images with lots of color changes in a small space, use JPEG. For graphics, line art, text, or logos, use GIF or PNG. Sometimes, you might want to try different formats to see which works best for you.

3 Choose the quality level. You can usually go down to 80% in a JPEG without any noticeable difference. You can often cut the quality much more without significantly hurting the image's appearance.

4 Check the file size and quality are both okay. You can see some extreme examples and a mid-way example below:

JPEG at 100% quality. File size: 201K

JPEG at 50% quality. File size: 46.5K

JPEG at 10% quality. File size: 27.4K

Beware

Don't overwrite your original file with a lower quality version, especially if you're using digital photos from your camera. Create a backup version of your photo first, and then edit that.

Hot tip

Reuse the same images on different web pages. The browser only needs to download them once, so your second page seems much faster.

47

Hot tip

If you're using small preview pictures (thumbnails) to link to larger images, it is acceptable to have a lower picture quality on the thumbnails, as long as the photos can still be identified.

Adding a map to your site

If you have a shop or office that you want people to visit, a map is essential. It's easy to add one using Google Maps:

1 Go to the Google Maps website (**http://maps.google. com**) and search for your address.

2 Use the zoom controls embedded in the left of the map to adjust the view, so that you can see as much detail as you want. Click + to zoom in.

48

Screenshots courtesy of Google. Map data copyright 2013 Google, Sanborn.

3 Click the link icon at the top of the left column. It looks like a chain. A new box will open. Click to customize your map and a new window will open, shown on the left.

4 Choose your map size. It's better to include a large map, and make enough room for it, than to try to squeeze a small map into a corner of your site. Customers will want to scroll around the map to work out their directions.

5 At the bottom of the screen, you'll see a box of HTML code. You'll learn how HTML works in Chapter 6. If you're not ready to use this code yet, it's okay to copy and paste it into a text file on your PC to keep it somewhere safe. Otherwise, paste it into your web page where you want the map to appear.

4 Layout and design

Your layout needs to communicate order and consistency, so the design looks professional and is easy to use. The fonts, colors, textures and images you choose will combine to create the look and feel of your website.

The role of your design

Don't be afraid to leave some empty space, at the bottom of a column, for example. It gives your design breathing space.

Now that you've spent some time planning and creating content, it's time to look at the layout and design of your web pages. Your website design needs to achieve the following goals:

- **Encourage engagement.** Your website design needs to inspire visitors to look around your site and spend some time there. It's easy to focus on this aspect of the design, but don't get carried away. Keep the purpose of your site in mind throughout its development, otherwise you might end up with something that is beautiful, but otherwise useless. Different styles will resonate with different audiences, which is why it's important to understand your target visitors first.

- **Communicate order.** Whether you have five pages or five hundred, your website design needs to make it easy for people to understand which pages are more important, and which parts of each page are most important.

- **Define the boundaries of the website.** Because people can move between websites so easily, it's important that they understand when this has happened. Using a consistent design across your web pages helps to reassure visitors that they are still on your website. You can create different layouts for different page types (your homepage and product pages are bound to look different, for example), but these should share the same design elements. Avoid using radically different color schemes or graphic styles on different pages, otherwise visitors might think they've gone to a different website. Anything that makes the visitor think about using your website, instead of just getting on with doing so, is a barrier to your site achieving its goals.

- **Feel easy-to-use.** Your site navigation needs to feel intuitive to visitors, so that they can easily find things. They want to spend time using your content, not trying to figure out how to find it. Navigation is so important that Chapter 5 is dedicated to it.

- **Inspire confidence.** If you have a site that visitors consider to be professionally designed, they're more likely to come back or spend money with you. People will (sometimes subconsciously) judge the quality of your expertise or services based on how professional your website looks.

Use whatever tools you find easiest. You could start with pen and paper, use an art package like Adobe Photoshop, or go straight into an HTML prototype.

Fixed or flexible?

One of the challenges of website design is that you don't know how large the user's web browser window will be. Screen sizes vary greatly, and people often resize their browser window so that they can see more than one application on screen, side by side.

The website design is typically contained in a box on the screen (a container box). Sometimes this box has no border, so it's invisible. But how the size of that box is defined governs what happens to the whole web page, at different screen and window sizes. There are several common strategies for dealing with the uncertainty of different screen and window sizes.

Fixed width design

Fixed width is perhaps the most popular solution to the challenge of different screen sizes. In a fixed width design, the container box has a width that is always the same size. This gives the designer the most control over the look of the final web page, so it makes it easier to create pages that consistently look good.

It takes control away from users, though. If they shrink the browser window, they might have to scroll horizontally as well as vertically to see everything, which is annoying. Users with big screens see the website at a smaller size than their screen could display, but the content remains easy to navigate and read.

On a smaller screen, there is less white space at the sides, and less of the page's height is visible at once. But the core design is preserved, and the web designer remains in control. The Guardian (**www.theguardian. com**) has built one of the many sites that use this strategy.

Hot tip

How wide should your fixed width design be? W3Counter (www.w3counter. com/globalstats. php) publishes screen resolution data based on visitors to over 69,000 websites. In September 2013, fewer than 2.71% of people still used 800 x 600 screens. Most desktop users had at least 1024 x 768 resolution. Designers often use a fixed width of 960 pixels, which leaves space for the scrollbar and other browser features. 960 is also easily divisible into columns.

Above: The Guardian website on a narrow monitor.

Left: The Guardian website on a wide monitor.

Hot tip

If you already have a website, use your web analytics to measure your visitors' screen resolutions.

...cont'd

Flexible design

In a flexible web design, the website design stretches or shrinks to the size of the browser window.

This strategy reduces the amount of scrolling users have to do, because the content can make optimal use of the screen space available. You can combine a flexible design with a maximum width, so that the site scales down for smaller screens and windows, but doesn't become too wide to read comfortably on large monitors. Flexible design can be hard to do well, because everybody sees a different amount of content on screen depending on the size of their monitor and/or browser window.

The Broads Authority (**www.broads-authority.gov.uk**) uses a flexible design with a maximum width. The content columns expand to use the available space, but the maximum width stops them from becoming too wide.

Variable content design

Some sites show additional content to users who have larger screens. This needs to be non-essential bonus content, because not everyone will see it. Amazon is a good example of this. Its main books page, for example, expands horizontally to show more books when viewed on a wider screen.

52

Using the grid

Web designers often use a grid to help them position content on screen, within the container box.

Grids are routinely used for designing print products. Newspapers, for example, use column-based layouts. Sometimes, a headline or a picture might span two, three or four columns. But it rarely spans two and a half columns, because that tends to look messy. Whether you're working in print or online, if you can line up blocks of content, it makes your design look tidier.

Take a look at the website for the Drupal content management system (**www.drupal.org**). The grey stripes have been overlaid to show the 12 column grid that is the foundation of this design.

The top blue section is divided into two halves. The first white section contains three boxes, all aligned to the same grid. Some of the content within these boxes is centered, but most of it sits tightly against the edge of the column. Towards the bottom of the page, the design is two-column again, and aligned to the same grid. Notice how well all the content on the left is aligned, from the logo down to the footer links.

Not everything has to sit rigidly on the grid: you can break out of it for emphasis, and to create some pace in the design. But, if nothing lines up, a web page can look amateurish or chaotic.

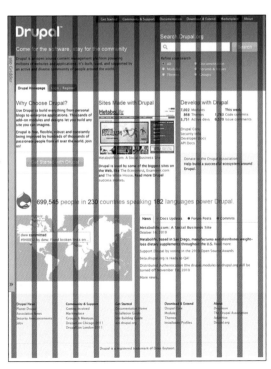

Hot tip

The free 960 Grid System (**www.960.gs**), developed by Nathan Smith, provides CSS templates you can use to help build your grid-based layout. It also includes sketch sheets you can print out to help you plan a 12, 16 or 24 column design.

Hot tip

To stop the design looking too blocky, don't put a border around all your content boxes.

Tips for good alignment

To ensure your web page lines up well, follow these steps:

1 Mark up your content correctly, using the right HTML tags, to identify a heading or a list item, for example. By default, HTML brings consistency, ensuring that all headlines and bullets line up. You'll learn more about HTML in Chapter 6.

2 Take care when adding spacing using CSS (changing the padding and margin around an element). This can introduce inconsistencies that throw out the natural alignment that HTML gives you. You'll learn how to control spacing using CSS in Chapter 7.

3 Be careful if you're using a visual editing system to build your web pages. They will often let you place content wherever you want on the page, but won't alert you if you're a few pixels out in lining things up. That can lead to designs that look sloppy.

4 It's easier to create a strong alignment, and the impression of good design that goes with it, if you align content with the left or right edge of the page or content box. If you center content, the alignment is harder to see. Centered paragraphs are also harder to read, because the start of each line is harder to find. Newcomers often want to center everything, but you should limit your use of center alignment to a few carefully selected parts of your design.

Right: The inconsistent alignment and center-aligned text looks messy.

Far right: The pictures line up with each other, the text above and the company name. The left-aligned main text looks cleaner. The footer is right-aligned with the right-margin of the main content box. This is far from a complete web design, but it does show the difference good alignment makes.

Thinking above the fold

As well as column based layouts, there's another idea the web has borrowed from the newspaper industry: the fold.

When broadsheet newspapers are laid out for sale, they're folded across the middle and only the top half can be seen. The bit that's on show is said to be "above the fold". Newspapers are designed to have their major headlines and photos in this top half of the page, so that people are drawn to them and pick up the paper. The newspaper's branding also appears prominently in this top half, so that people can recognise it immediately.

In web design, the term "above the fold" is used to refer to the first screenful of content. It's what people can see without having to scroll the page, so it is their first impression of your website. It's essential that your website's identity or branding, and its navigation, appears above the fold. By having multiple columns of text, you can also start several different stories above the fold and invite people to click to read more or scroll down the page to finish reading.

Of course, the fold doesn't appear at the same place for everyone. It varies depending on the screen resolution, browser used, and the number of browser toolbars in use. If you're assuming a minimum screen height of 768 pixels, a good place to think of the fold is being 575-590 pixels down the page. But remember that this is the minimum and that people will see lots of different sized screenfuls.

People don't always notice the scrollbar, so you need to provide a visual cue to encourage people to scroll down the page. An easy way to do this is to box some of the content, and stagger where the boxes end. People will understand that if they can't see the bottom border of the box, they haven't seen everything.

About us	About us
• Careers • What we do • Contact • Terms • Press • Location	Lorem ipsum dolor sit amet, consectetuer adipiscing elit. Maecenas porttitor congue massa. Fusce posuere, magna sed pulvinar ultricies, purus lectus malesuada libero, sit amet commodo magna eros quis urna.
Other countries	Nunc viverra imperdiet enim. Fusce est. Vivamus a tellus.
• Germany • France • Spain • Italy	Pellentesque habitant morbi tristique senectus et netus et malesuada fames ac turpis egestas. Proin pharetra nonummy pede. Mauris et orci.

About us	About us
• Careers • What we do • Contact • Terms • Press • Location	Lorem ipsum dolor sit amet, consectetuer adipiscing elit. Maecenas porttitor congue massa. Fusce posuere, magna sed pulvinar ultricies, purus lectus malesuada libero, sit amet commodo magna eros quis urna.
Other countries	Nunc viverra imperdiet enim. Fusce est. Vivamus a tellus.
• Germany • France • Spain • Italy	Pellentesque habitant morbi tristique senectus et netus et malesuada fames ac turpis egestas. Proin pharetra nonummy pede. Mauris et orci.

Far left: The user has no clue that this page continues below the fold (the red line).

Left: Boxing the left column tells the user the web page continues below the fold, prompting them to scroll.

Organizing information

Within each web page, you need to create a hierarchy of information. It needs to be easy for visitors to see what's most important on any given page, and easy for them to skim-read the page to find what they're looking for.

Think of it like a newspaper. The size of the headlines, and their position on the page, tells you a lot about the relative importance of different stories.

Here are some tips for organizing the content on your web page:

● Larger text looks more important than smaller text.

● Things higher up the page tend to be more important than things further down the page.

● Be consistent. If you have 20 different sizes of text, it will be difficult for people to gauge their relative importance. Use up to three different types of headings which are consistently formatted. Using the HTML <h1> to <h3> tags correctly will enforce consistency by default.

● Use bulleted lists and subheadings to structure your content. You can create them using HTML, so they're part of the language of navigating the web.

● You can use contrasting color or spacing around elements to call attention to them. Video on demand company LoveFilm (**www.lovefilm.com**), for example, could use a text link to bring people into its subscription process. But it uses a bright green button with space around it, so that there's no mistaking the most important action on this page.

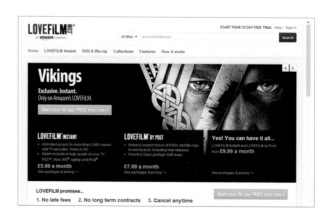

Creating a color scheme

The typical computer can display millions of colors, so how do you choose a handful that work well? The good news is that there are lots of tools that encapsulate the important color design theories, and they're often free. Here's a suggested approach:

CoffeeCup Website Color Schemer is a dedicated commercial tool (**www. coffeecup.com**)

1 Think of a starting color. You could take it from your company logo, your favorite color, or from the association of a color with a particular meaning or mood. Red spells danger or romance, green references nature, and blue communicates stability, for example. If you have an image that will be a prominent part of your design, you could take the color from that. The pipette tool in Photoshop can be used to grab a color from a photo, so you can find out its RGB color number.

Change the personality of your palette by using tints and shades. You get a tint when you add white to a color. You get a shade when you add black to a color.

2 Open a color scheme tool. You can find one at **www.colorschemedesigner.com**, and Adobe has one called Kuler at **http://kuler.adobe.com**. You might have one built in to your web design software or image editing software.

Color wheels encapsulate important design theories. If you just make up your own set of colors, without reference to the color wheel, there's a good chance they'll clash.

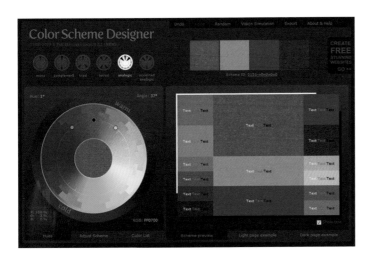

...cont'd

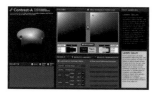

Above: Contrast-A, by Das Plankton, offers much more in-depth analysis of contrast. It's free to use at **http://www.dasplankton.de/ContrastA/**

Hot tip

Don't be afraid to use black on white for large areas of text. It offers the best contrast, so it's easy to read. Most of the major websites (including search engines, news sites, shops, and social networks) use black text on a white background for their core content.

Right: The Color Contrast Checker helps you make sure your foreground and background colors make a legible combination.

3 Choose your starting color. You usually do this by clicking it on a color wheel. Using Kuler, you can also type in a hex value of the color or its RGB value.

4 Choose what type of color scheme you would like to create. You have several options here. A monochromatic scheme uses shades of one color. A complementary scheme uses two colors that are directly opposite each other on the color wheel. A triad uses three colors that are the same distance apart on the wheel. There's also a split complement triad, which uses one color, and the two colors beside its complement on the other side of the wheel. An analogous color scheme uses colors that are next to each other on the color wheel. Experiment to see what works well for you.

5 Note the color numbers in the palette provided. You'll need to put them in your CSS code later.

6 To make sure that your site is easy for everyone to read, it's important to make sure there is enough contrast between your foreground and background colors. Take a screengrab of your color combination (text on background) and then use an art package to make it grayscale, to see how legible it is. Alternatively, enter your colors into the Color Contrast Check at **http://snook.ca/technical/colour_contrast/colour.html** It will tell you whether your colors comply with accessibility guidelines.

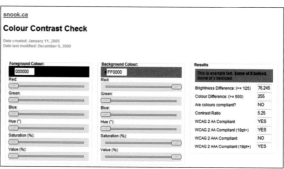

Using gradients

Solid blocks of color can be overwhelming, if the color is a warm one like red or yellow, or might just look a bit flat if not. That's why websites often use a gradient instead, where one color fades into another. One simple way to do this is to create a background image that represents part of the gradient, and then repeat it.

For example, this stripe of color:

is set as a repeating background on the website for web surfing game Wild Mood Swings (**www.wildmoodswings.co.uk**), like this:

You can use a gradient to soften any area of color. Firetask (**www.firetask.com**) uses a gradient for its blue background, and fades it into the white that is used for the content. The blue background dominates the first screenful, and might have been overwhelming without the gradient.

Firetask also uses shades of blue for its logo, navigation bar and Buy Now buttons, creating a sense of harmony and continuity in the design.

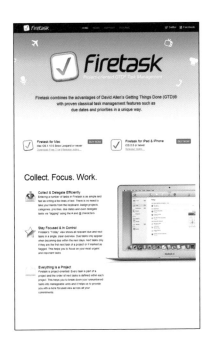

You can also use an image to add texture to your page. You could use a photo of wood or a wall, or something more subtle, like sand. Harmony Republic (**www.harmonyrepublic. com**) uses a texture like stained paper.

You can also use CSS to add simple gradients to your design with a few text commands. There are online generators you can use to make the code, including at **http:// www.colorzilla.com/ gradient-editor/** and **http://www.cssmatic. com/gradient-generator**

Choosing fonts

The style of text you use on your website has a huge impact on its design. Some fonts are playful, some are business-like; some speak of tradition, while others look futuristic. All this information is conveyed before somebody has even read what the text says.

You should use fonts that convey the personality of your site, where possible, although there are lots of technical limitations on this. When the web browser displays text, it uses the fonts on the visitor's PC. That means you're limited to a relatively small set of safe fonts if you want everyone to see the same thing.

However, you can give the browser a list of font options, so you could request a daring and relatively rare font and give the browser a safe substitute if that font isn't available. You could use a font that comes with Adobe Creative Suite or Microsoft Office, for people who have those packages, for example, and declare a basic font that comes with the operating system, as a back-up.

Harrington

Jokerman

Old English Text

Palace Script

Rage Italic

Ravie

ROSEWOOD STD

Snap ITC

STENCIL STD

For small pieces of text, such as a headline, you could create a picture that shows the text and put that in your web page. That approach is always used for logos, and could also be used for small headlines, but it should be used selectively. It makes your web page slower to load, creates a lot of work for you, in building and editing the site, and makes it harder for search engines and users of assistive technology to understand your content. If you're using Flash, you can embed a font in your Flash file, too, so you can send the font over the Internet with your content.

Pay attention to the size of the text and its color. Some fonts look good at larger sizes but not at smaller, and vice versa. You can use color to change how heavy the font looks on screen, too. A big blocky font can be softened by changing its color from black to blue, for example.

What is your look and feel?

The look and feel of your website is what results from all the decisions you make about its content and design.

It is a combination of:

- The images you use. Both the style of your content images and photography, and the choice and arrangement of any decorative images.

- The attitude suggested by your text, and the language it uses.

- The color scheme you have chosen.

- The fonts you use to convey your information and draw attention to important elements.

- The way you arrange elements on the page to accentuate what is important.

Hot tip

Professionals often create the look and feel in an art package, like Photoshop. They make an image of the whole web page. This image can then be sliced up to make the background and foreground images that will form part of the finished website.

You need all these elements to work in harmony. If you were promoting an industrial rock band and had lots of metallic textured images, it would look strange to have a fancy handwritten font, or lots of bright kid-friendly colors. Sometimes you can subvert conventional wisdom, but it's usually better to play it safe.

Using design elements consistently sends a signal to your visitors that you've paid attention to the details. It's easy to put things onto a screen. It takes more care to combine them so that they look like they belong together in a single design. Work within a palette of four or five colors (plus shades or tints, as appropriate). Make the spacing between different elements on your web page consistent. Choose one or two fonts and use them throughout.

The rule of thumb is: if things look similar, they should be exactly the same. If they're nearly the same, it just looks sloppy. If you don't want things to look the same, then make them radically different. Leave no doubt that you have deviated from the norm to add contrast or emphasis, or to call attention to something.

When you're developing the elements of your look and feel, keep your intended audience in mind. Think about the kinds of magazines they read, the TV shows they might watch, the films they prefer, and their favorite websites (until yours is built, at least). Use a visual language that will make them feel at home.

The right look and feel

To understand the importance of the look and feel, here are three websites that cater for different audiences. I've chosen obviously contrasting examples, but you can see that if you swapped the design of these websites around, their audiences would be put off using the sites.

The website for Seventeen (**www.seventeen.com**), a magazine for teenage girls, uses a pink, blue and green color scheme on white. To bring readers into the features, it has text-based navigation that is easy to skim read.

Saga (**www.saga.co.uk**) offers services including insurance and holidays to the over 50s. The homepage is clear and easy to navigate. It has a conservative blue and white color scheme. To help those with poor vision, it has an option to enlarge the text.

The Moshi Monsters website (**www.moshimonsters.com**) is designed for children. It uses text sparingly and keeps the language simple. There are few navigation options, which are shown using memorable icons. The color palette is bold and exciting, and Flash is used to animate characters in the town scene.

Beware

Don't let brand guidelines constrain you into creating a poor web experience. Sometimes there's a conflict between a company's brand and what works well on the web. Large companies often revise their offline brand guidelines for consistency with the website, rather than forcing the web to adopt a style that was developed for print. Many companies believe the most important thing is that the website offers a consistent experience that is an extension of the brand, and not necessarily that it replicates the printed materials.

Don't forget

You don't have to use guesswork. You can invite members of your audience to give you feedback on every stage of your design.

5 Designing effective navigation

Effective navigation will help your visitors to understand your site structure, to find what they need, and to explore everything your website has to offer. In this chapter, I'll share some guidelines and technical tips to help you create effective navigation.

Good navigation is important for search engines, too. They will follow the links on your site (or "crawl it"), to discover all your web pages.

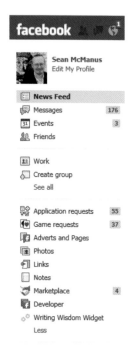

Above: Facebook's navigation bar, providing access to the different features of the site.

What is navigation?

Navigation is all about the links you provide to enable people to move between the different parts and pages of your website. Your navigation needs to address four key challenges:

- Visitors won't know what's on your website unless you tell them. Entire sections of your site could be overlooked if people don't know they're there.

- People don't have the patience or commitment to try to work out how to use your website. They just want to be able to understand it immediately, and want to intuitively know how to get around it. If they can't work out where to find something they want, they'll probably leave your website altogether.

- People don't know how your website is structured unless you tell them. They want to feel that they understand where they are in the whole site, not to feel like they're bouncing between pages aimlessly.

- Visitors will want to take a different path through your website, depending on their interests. You can't assume or expect that everyone will want to view your web pages in the same order.

It is possible, and desirable, to put links anywhere in your content. If a blog post mentions your latest product, then you should link to it so that people can find out more information easily. Providing links in context at the time people might want them makes it much easier for people to explore your website.

When people think of navigation, though, they usually think of those links that are separated from the content that provide access to everything the site offers. A group of links at the top or the side of the page is often called a "navigation bar", or a "navbar" for short. Because it's separated from the page content, it's easy to spot, and it often uses design elements that draw attention to it.

It's risky to copy another site's navigation, because what works for them won't necessarily work for you. That said, there are certain conventions that you need to take into account. Visitors arrive with some opinions of how a website should work, based on all the other websites they've used. If you can meet their expectations, they'll find it easier to use your site, and you'll find it easier to keep their interest.

Laying out your navigation

You might think that every website looks different, but if you look closely, you'll see that there's often a lot of overlap in where navigation options are placed on websites. You can use this to your advantage: by borrowing from this consensus, you can make it easier for your visitors to understand how to use your website.

Here's a pattern you can use for placing your navigation options:

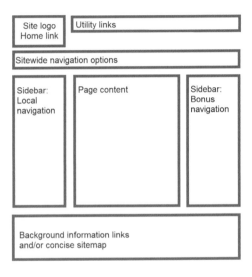

- Your site logo in the top left corner links to the homepage.

- Your sitewide navigation options are below the logo, or to the side of it. These will be the main links to different sections on your site, such as different types of products. In most sites, these links remain the same across every page of the site. In extremely large sites, these can change depending on the page the visitor is viewing, but they remain the most important links. This navbar should be immediately obvious. Its location helps communicate its role, but you can help it stand out by using larger text, contrasting color or spacing around it.

- Utility links are placed in the top right corner. These are tools for using the site, so are separated from the content sections or product categories in the sitewide navbar. Utility links might include My Account, Log In, Help, Customer Service, Contact Us, Privacy Policy, and Search.

Beware

This is only a pattern: it doesn't work for every website. If it doesn't work for yours, don't try to force your website into it.

Hot tip

Some of your web pages might fit equally well in more than one category. About Us, for example, could be a utility or a background link for the footer. It's up to you how to categorize links, but it's a good idea to keep similar links together. If you also have links for Careers and Press Releases, About Us belongs with them, wherever they are.

..cont'd

Above: The retailer Asda Direct (**http://direct. asda.com**) matches the pattern without a right sidebar. Utility links include Track your Order and Register; the logo links to home; the main navbar provides access to the different types of product (e.g. Entertainment); the left sidebar provides links that are relevant to the current section (e.g. Dance CDs, Rock CDs); and the footer provides background links (Careers, Returns Policy, Privacy).

- The left sidebar is used for navigation options that are relevant to the section the visitor is in. For example, if they are in the book section, they might see different genres here.

- The right sidebar is used for bonus navigation options, such as tag clouds (see Encouraging Exploration later in this chapter) or links to the latest blog comments from visitors.

- The box across the bottom is used for links to background information about the website (such as About Us, Press Releases, Investor Information), and/or to provide a short sitemap with links into the main sections on the site and their most important subsections.

No site exactly matches this pattern, of course. It's a generalization. Many websites will only have one sidebar, either the left or the right one, and some will have none at all. The sidebars often include other content, too, such as advertisements.

Some websites don't have a horizontal navigation bar across the top, and put all their navigation options down the side. But it's a useful crib sheet to help you design your navigation, because it will feel intuitive to visitors.

The pattern also ensures that the most important links have due prominence. All the important navigation options should be immediately obvious when the page loads.

A sitemap at the bottom of the page gives readers somewhere to go when they've finished reading an article, and the main navigation has been scrolled off the top of the screen.

Which links belong where depends on your site, but there are a couple of guidelines:

- The shopping basket is often placed in the top right corner, with the utilities, or on the right of the sitewide navbar.

- A link to the homepage (where present) should be the first item in any navbar.

- The search box can be placed almost anywhere, as long as it's obvious what it is. It's often seen in the top right, in the sitewide navbar, or at the top of the left or right sidebar.

Grouping the options

A navbar's job is to create order and provide direction. That's not always easy: when the site has diverse content or is large, it can be difficult to summarize it through a handful of links.

Take a look at the list of nine links on the left below, for example. It might cover everything that's on the site, but is it easy to use? Not particularly. Long lists of links are hard for people to skim-read, so people have to slow down to use them. That makes the site feel laborious to navigate.

Fixing it is easy. The links can be grouped into three sections: Shop, Free downloads and About us. By putting a small heading above these links, it's easy to see at a glance what's on the site.

Beware

The art of navigation design is to strike a balance between the number of clicks required to get somewhere, and making it obvious what the next click should be for any given visitor. You could put a link to every page on your homepage, which would enable everywhere to be reached in one click. But nobody wants to try to make sense of 150 links. At the other extreme, if you only give people one option from a page, they'll know where to click but will get frustrated at the lack of choice and control over their visit.

Before grouping

- Books
- CDs
- Posters
- Wallpapers
- MP3s
- Who we are
- Team photos
- Visiting us
- Contact us

After grouping

Shop
- Books
- CDs
- Posters

Free downloads
- Wallpapers
- MP3s

About us
- Who we are
- Team photos
- Visiting us
- Contact us

Whether you are creating vertical navigation or horizontal navigation, the secret of making it work is to group your links in a way that makes intuitive sense to your visitors, and then to communicate that grouping. If you've invested time in planning your sitemap first, you'll find it much easier to do this.

You could use these links with subheadings in the sidebar or the footer, or you could create a horizontal navbar with buttons for Shop, Free Downloads and About Us. When people click those, you could take them into a page with more options for the subcategories, or you could start showing them selected content, and provide links to the different subcategories on the left.

Some people say that you should be able to get anywhere on the site within three clicks. It's a helpful guideline, but the most important thing is that people can easily find what they need and feel that they are getting closer to it with every click. Arranging links in easily understood groups helps to achieve that.

You can also have dropdown menus that come out from the side of a menu option. In this case, they usually fly out to the right of a button. eBay (www.ebay.com) uses this technique:

Dropdown menus

Dropdown navigation enables people to get to many more web pages in a single click, without clogging the screen up with too many links.

A dropdown menu usually opens when somebody puts the mouse over an option on the navigation bar, providing immediate access to some of the subpages under that option. If somebody puts the mouse over About Us, for example, a dropdown menu might appear with options for Contact Us and Recruitment.

The user can click those options, or can ignore the dropdown menu and click the button on the navbar. It's important that this continues to work, otherwise people who can't see the dropdown menu (because it doesn't work on their browser) won't have any navigation options at all. The navbar shouldn't be there just to open the dropdown menu.

Fuel Your Creativity (**www.fuelyourcreativity.com**) uses a dropdown menu. As you can see in the screenshot below, the menu appears to be in front of the site content, so it doesn't take up any additional screen space. When the mouse is moved out of the menu, it closes again.

The site also uses a tooltip, a box that appears near the user's cursor, to remind people they can still click the main navbar to view all the content in that section. Because tooltips aren't visible all the time, and some people will never trigger their display, you shouldn't depend on them to explain navigation. But you can use them to offer additional advice.

Dropdown menus are sometimes called pop-up menus, or pulldown menus. Pulldown menus usually require a click to open them.

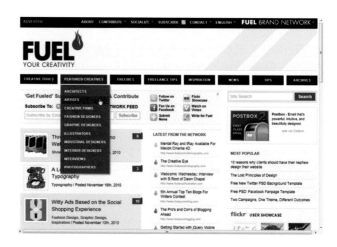

...cont'd

Inkd (**www.inkd.com**), a website for buying and selling graphic design templates, uses tabs for its navigation, combined with a dropdown menu. It has a downward pointing arrow on the right of each tab, which opens the dropdown menu when the cursor moves over it. The arrows give visitors a hint that there are menus they can open. Often, people don't know a dropdown menu is available until it appears.

Beware

Touchscreen devices can't detect a cursor hovering over a particular place on the screen. The finger is either touching the screen or it isn't. Apple devices use the first touch to trigger the action of a cursor hovering, but some other devices might not handle dropdown menus well.

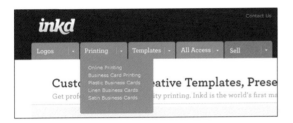

The mega dropdown works like a dropdown menu, but instead of displaying a single column of links, it shows many columns of options. These need to be designed with care, to ensure they can be easily scanned by visitors and are not overwhelming. People skim-read lists vertically, so, if you sort the options alphabetically, arrange them in columns and not rows. Within the mega dropdown box, you can also use headings to identify groups of links, so that people can find what they want more quickly.

MTV (**www.mtv.com**) uses a mega dropdown. As you can see, when you roll the mouse over Shows, a panel full of options opens. The program names are sorted alphabetically in columns.

Hot tip

Alphabetical sorting is ideal for links where their title is unambiguous, such as the name of a band or TV show. If people might not know what you've called a particular category, or it could be one of several things, alphabetical sorting might not add enough structure to make your list intuitive.

Use Google image search to find icon sets. It returns images showing all (or most of) the icons in a set.

Make sure your icons are big enough to be clear. An icon that is obvious to you, after seeing it throughout the development project, might not be so obvious to the strangers it is there to help.

Right: Dryicons (www. dryicons.com) offers a wide range of free and paid icon sets in diverse styles and colors. Each set includes icons for different processes or pages of your website, designed in a consistent but distinctive style. Dryicons' icon sets can be as large as hundreds of icons, but typically comprise 20 or 50.

Using icons

One way to call attention to important links and information is to create a representative icon for them. Icons can be a useful visual shorthand that enable people to quickly see where they should click, as well as making it easier for them to do so by increasing the size of the link on screen.

There are lots of symbols and metaphors from the real world that are often used on websites. For example:

- From the class room, a green tick is often used to indicate that a form field has been completed correctly, with a red cross marking an error.

- The symbols used on a DVD player's remote control are often used for online media: a triangle pointing right represents play, a square means stop, and two triangles fast forward back or forwards, depending on the direction they point.

- From the supermarket, a shopping cart is used to represent the page that shows the products the visitor wants to buy.

- From the postal service, an envelope is often used to represent email or contact information.

- Arrows pointing left and right are often used to represent the next or previous stage in a process, respectively.

Lots of professional designers make their icons available for free use on other websites in exchange for a link, or sell a commercial license to those who don't want to link.

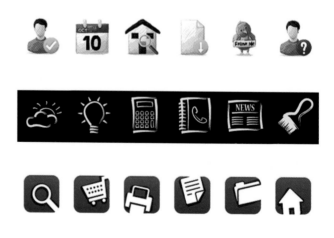

Tabbed navigation

One navigation metaphor that is sometimes used for the main navigation is to simulate the effect of tab pages in a ring binder. When you click a tab on a web page, the idea is that it should look like you have brought its page to the front of the screen.

Here is an example created using a free demonstration file from **www.dhtmlgoodies.com**:

| Articles | Books | Shop | About us |

Scratch Programming in Easy Steps

Scratch is a programming language that's widely ｜ schools and universities, and is the perfect first point for people of all ages who want to learn to program. It's designed to enable you to be creati

The metaphor is well understood by visitors, and can be effective in defining the boundaries of different sections of your website. To make the most of the tabbed navigation metaphor:

- Make sure you create the illusion of the tab being joined to the page below. You can do this by using the same color on the tab and the content beneath it, and a contrasting color on other tabs. It's okay to change the color of a tab to highlight that it is the current page.

- Have one of your tabs selected when people arrive at the homepage, to show the metaphor working from the start of their visit.

- Make sure that the text is clear and legible on every tab. If there isn't room to make the tabs big enough to be clear, then restructure the navigation. Don't shrink the text.

- Use spacing between the tabs and rounded corners on them, to create a sense of separation between your website sections.

As with any navbar, your tabbed navigation should look and work consistently across the website.

Good navigation is invisible. People just use it without noticing it. Only when the navigation is frustrating do people pay it much attention. So, when you're online, think about the navigation you see and what works well. You can use this knowledge to craft your own navigation design.

There are lots of tools and templates online that you can use to help you to create menus and navigation.

The role of the homepage

The homepage has a special role to play in your site's navigation. As the page that people see when they type in your domain name, it's the official first page of your website. Visitors expect it to introduce them to what the site's about, and give them some pointers towards content they might want to explore.

If somebody follows a link from another site or search engine, the first page they see might be deep within one of your content sections. If they feel lost, they know they can visit the homepage to reorientate themselves.

There is a simple convention in website design that you should follow to make this easy: put your company or site logo in the top left corner of the screen, and make it a link to the homepage. It helps to add a "Home" link to your navbar, too, perhaps with an icon of a house to represent it.

Hot tip

If your site has a lot of content, you might need to have intermediate navigation pages to help people navigate each section. These pages can perform a role similar to what the homepage does for the whole website, introducing the section and enabling people to start exploring its contents. Smaller websites can take people directly from the homepage to the content pages.

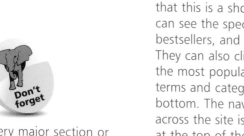

Don't forget

Every major section or product category on your website should be represented on the homepage.

Right: The Barnes & Noble homepage (**www.bn.com**) gives people lots of ways in to the site, and leaves no doubt that this is a shop. Shoppers can see the special offers, bestsellers, and newest books. They can also click links for the most popular search terms and categories at the bottom. The navigation used across the site is introduced at the top of the page. Nearly all the screen space on this homepage is a link that entices people deeper into the website.

Your homepage should include:

- **A short, clear statement explaining what the site is about.** Write a short paragraph near the top of the page. Provide an About Us page for the detail.

- **Navigation options that help people find content relevant to them.** Depending on how your site is structured, you could use short snippets of articles with links to the full stories; selected products; or links to the different categories. While most pages of your site will be dominated by content, the homepage can be almost full of these navigation options.

- **A prominent search box.** Some people are happy to click around the site exploring, but many people want to search. The search box should be near the top of the screen. It's often placed on the right hand side.

- **The standard navigation bar.** Because people understand the homepage is different to other pages, you can get away with not having the same layout and navigation bar. But, if you standardize navigation from the homepage onwards, you can start teaching visitors how to navigate your site from the very first page.

Fiction writers are always advised to "show, not tell". In many ways, the same applies to your homepage. People only need enough context to get started. Don't tell people you have lots of special offers. Show them the offers. Don't tell people you enable them to watch videos. Put your most popular video on the page and let them stop reading, and start watching. The goal of your homepage is to get people to start interacting with your site, not to be an instruction manual for it.

Hot tip

People particularly like to see timely content on the homepage. Include links to your latest blog posts, press releases, or products there. Update your homepage often, to show the site is lively.

73

Left: Google's first homepage from 1998, courtesy of The Wayback Machine (**web.archive. org**). Google has always let its search results speak for the company. The 1998 homepage enables you to search the web, with links for more information if you need it. Google is famous enough now to have dropped the "search the web" instructions. But they have always led by showing, not telling.

Don't forget

If you're using tabbed navigation, you can highlight the current tab to show people where they are in the site.

Hot tip

Don't remove the current page from the navbar. You might think it's illogical to offer a link to where the visitor already is, but people get more confused if the navbar changes shape or links move around in it, which is what happens when you remove links. As far as possible, your navbar should be standardized so that people can easily learn how to use it.

You are here...

One of the goals of your navigation is to show people where they are in the site. That provides context to help them understand the content, and also helps them to build a mental map of how big your site is, and which sections they have already explored.

There are lots of different techniques you can use to help people understand their place in your website. The more hints you can give visitors, the easier they will understand your site structure.

Give each page a title

Every page of the site should have a title that appears immediately above its content. The title should uniquely identify that page, and help people to understand its purpose. On a news article, the title might be the story headline. Reassure visitors that the navigation is working well by making your page title similar to the text on any links to that page. If people click a link and arrive at a page with an unexpected title, it can be confusing.

Change the color of visited links

For your text links, you can have the color of visited links automatically changed by the browser, so that people can understand where they have already been (see Chapter 7).

Change the navbar

Show people which section of the site they are in by changing its appearance on the navbar. Remember that people might not have clicked a link on the navbar to get there. They might have used a link in the middle of your page content, or a link on another site altogether. Cartoonist Scott McCloud (**www.scottmccloud.com**) uses lines from the icon to show the current section.

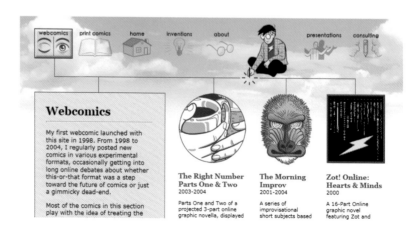

Using breadcrumb trails

Breadcrumb trails reveal the primary path through the website, by showing how the current page relates to other pages above it in the hierarchy. They don't necessarily show how somebody got to the page they are on: they just show the main route there.

The different levels of the hierarchy are typically separated with greater than signs, and each level is clickable, so that people can easily jump up one or two levels. The last item in the trail is the current page, which shouldn't be a link because you're already there. For example, a breadcrumb trail might look like this:

<u>Home</u> > <u>Books</u> > <u>Computing</u> > Web Design in easy steps

For many sites, the breadcrumb trail can be a good way to show the site structure, and enable easy navigation within a section. It only works when each page can only sit within a single category, and it isn't intuitive enough to be used on its own. Consider breadcrumb trails to be a bonus feature to improve usability, rather than your primary navigation. To make it easy to understand, write "You are here" before the trail, and place it at the top of the web page.

Creating a process map

There is one place on the site where it's often considered acceptable to remove navigation altogether. That's when people are filling out a form to complete a process, such as registration or a purchase. The site owners don't want people to be distracted by other content on the site, so they focus their attention by removing all other options. Of course, this can be annoying for the customer if they decide they want to go and add something else to the shopping cart. But it can also be helpful by making the whole process easier to navigate and understand.

Create a map to show people where they are in the process, and how many steps there are to come. Amazon's appears at the top of the screen during the checkout process, with the current stage shown in bold, and future stages shown in gray.

Hot tip

Make sure your process map helps people to see their progress through the process. Update it at each stage, so that people are motivated to continue through to completion.

75

amazon.co.uk

WELCOME **ADDRESS** ITEMS WRAP DISPATCH PAY CONFIRM

Be careful with using explorative navigation. It should be a bonus feature of the site, not a replacement for navigation that provides immediate access to key content.

Encouraging exploration

It's essential to make it easy for people to find what they want, with clear navigation. But you should also inspire them to dig deeper, and to explore the potential of your site. Sometimes, you can make this a playful feature of the navigation.

The website for the Lego Batman game (**http://games.kidswb. com/official-site/lego-batman/**) has a cityscape, which visitors can scroll left and right to explore. As well as a frightful cast of villains scattered about the rooftops, there are Lego bricks that can be collected and stacked up, and features that appear when the mouse hovers over a doorway or other feature. It's never a good idea to make visitors hunt for links, so these are additional bonus links. For those who don't want to explore, there is a plain navbar underneath the scrolling window.

Designer Coen Grift (**www.bio-bak.nl**) has a clever design that encourages visitors to explore his surreal portfolio. The on-screen arm is your pointer, as you click and drag the mouse to move around the portfolio. Characters pop up and set tasks, such as finding tools scattered about the landscape. The homepage includes direct links to the biography, contact and awards pages so that people don't struggle to find the essential content.

The key ingredient in both these sites is fun. If it's entertaining, people will spend time playing with it. If it's not, they'll just get frustrated.

..cont'd

Both these sites are designed using Flash, but many text-led websites also incorporate features to encourage exploration.

Amazon uses its understanding of what customers like, its product database, and its instinct about products that are related because they're often bought by the same person. With that information, it is able to personalize link suggestions to customers.

When you visit Amazon, assuming you're logged in, most of the homepage is personalized to you. The site uses several different ways to present items that are related to products you've viewed, either recently or further back in your browsing history. It recommends products based on your browsing history, and shows your browsing history and wishlist so you can return to products you might now be ready to buy. The homepage also shows Amazon's promotions for its most important products, seasonal promotions, and the bestselling products in certain categories.

These features require a lot of data and sophisticated programming, and aren't justified by the size of most websites. But any site could learn from these ideas. You could easily enhance your product page with links to related products, or post links to your most popular pages in the margin of every page. Help people to explore your site and they're more likely to stick around long enough to find something they want to buy.

Hot tip

A tag cloud is a box of phrases where the size of each phrase reflects how often it's been used. Tag clouds are often used on blogs, so that people can get a quick snapshot of the topics the blog covers most often, and can navigate to the posts that cover those topics.

1 birthday blue bw california canada rope family festival flower flowers foc apan london music nature nev arty people photography portrait red sanfra van travel trip uk usa vacation wa

Hot tip

Content management systems and blogging platforms will often include the tag clouds, related posts, and other explorative navigation features.

Adding a search engine

A search engine is an essential navigation feature for any but the smallest website. People don't want to trawl through links hunting for something specific: they want to just ask the computer to find it for them. You can add a Google search engine to any website:

1 Go to **www.google.com/cse** and click the button to add a custom search engine. You will need to log in with your Google account, or create a new one if you don't already have one.

2 Into the box of sites to search, put your domain name, such as **www.example.com**, followed by /*. This will search the whole site. If you only want to include specific pages, you can list their full URLs here (for example, **www.example.com/books.html**) instead.

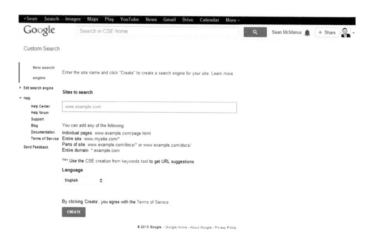

3 When you enter a URL, a new box appears so you can add another one. If you have more than one website, you can add all their URLs to make a search engine that returns results from them all.

4 Click the Create button at the bottom of the page.

5 Click the button to get the code. Copy it and paste it into your web page HTML, where you would like your search engine to appear.

6 Open the web page in your browser and test the search engine by typing in some keywords that should deliver pages from different parts of your website. The results appear in an overlay on top of your web page.

Hot tip

If you're a member of Google Adsense (**www.google.com/adsense**), Google will pay you when your site visitors click on the adverts in your search results.

7 Use the navigation options on the left if you want to change the settings of your search engine. The look and feel settings enable you to show search results on a different webpage to the one that hosts the search box. The search features enable you to add promotions that show specific pages in response to keywords.

This will only work if you are using an Apache server and you have permission from your hosting company to change the .htaccess file. Seek technical support if you can't make it work: this is a tricky feature.

Effective error messages

Sometimes things don't work out as they should, and you have to break the bad news to the visitor. Be gentle. In particular, avoid using language that accuses them of making a mistake or makes them feel like they've broken the site, when it almost certainly isn't their fault. It's better to offer practical advice on what they need to do next.

A common error happens when you move or remove a web page, resulting in what's known as a 404 error when somebody tries to visit it. You can customize the 404 error page, so that it helps to bring people back in to your site, rather than representing a dead end, which encourages them to leave. Follow these steps:

1. Create your error page. Use your normal site template to reassure people they are still in your site and provide links to your homepage, and most popular pages. Your links need to have the full URL, such as **http://www.example. com/news.html**, instead of just news.html. Include a search box. Save the page as 404message.html

2. Create a text file called htaccess.txt. This file only needs to contain one line:
   ErrorDocument 404 /404message.html

3. Upload your htaccess.txt and 404message.html files to the top level of your server using FTP (see Chapter 14). Rename htaccess.txt on the server to .htaccess (a dot then "htaccess", with nothing before the dot).

4. Test it by trying to visit a page you know doesn't exist. If all's gone well, you will see your customized error page!

Right: An error page on the BBC website, with advice to check the website address was typed correctly, search the site or use the site index.

14 tips for effective links

Here are some principles that will help ensure your links are easy for everybody to use, whatever device or browser they prefer:

1 Be consistent. Don't use different names to refer to the same section of your website. Even using easily interchanged terms, like "store" and "shop", to refer to the same section can create the impression that you couldn't make up your mind about what to call it.

2 Avoid quirky names for sections on your site. People won't waste time clicking to see where they go. Use simple terms like "Forum", "Shop" and "Reviews".

3 Keep the text in your links short. The links should be signposts to other pages, not lengthy descriptions of them.

4 Make sure your links make sense in isolation. They draw the eye on screen, and screenreaders often read links in isolation to help visitors see what they can do on the web page. Links that say "click here" or "more..." help nobody.

5 Don't have links sharing the same text, unless they go to the same page.

6 Make sure your link text is descriptive enough so that people can understand what they might find behind it before they click. People will get frustrated if they click a link to find that they're not interested in what's behind it.

7 Don't tell people where to click. It should be obvious, and if it isn't, redesign the navigation so that it is. If you want to provide help in context, don't say "click the Reviews button to find out more". Instead, provide a direct additional link to the reviews section.

8 Don't draw attention to the interface. Instead of saying "Click here to order the book", edit your link text so it is a strong call to action, for example: "Order the book". People already know they have to click that link to do so.

Search engines use the text on links to help them understand what the linked page is about. So using clear, descriptive text in your links helps with your search engine positioning, too.

Having too many links on a page can be overwhelming. The idea is to highlight some options people can take from the page they are on. Don't try to show them how they can reach every page from where they are in a single click.

...cont'd

What's the most important navigation tool on any website? The browser's back button. So avoid any tricks that stop it from working, such as immediately diverting people to a different web page using JavaScript.

Hot tip

Test your links regularly. Broken links frustrate visitors and are seen as a sign of poor quality by search engines. There's a free link checker at http://validator.w3.org/checklink

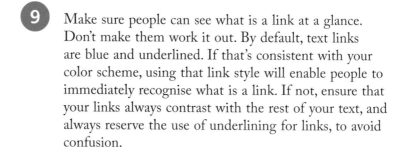

9 Make sure people can see what is a link at a glance. Don't make them work it out. By default, text links are blue and underlined. If that's consistent with your color scheme, using that link style will enable people to immediately recognise what is a link. If not, ensure that your links always contrast with the rest of your text, and always reserve the use of underlining for links, to avoid confusion.

10 Use plain HTML links (see Chapter 6) wherever possible. Humans and search engines alike might struggle to use JavaScript or Flash-based links.

11 If you link to something that isn't a standard web page, such as a PDF file, warn people by putting the name of the format in brackets towards the end of the link text. For example, you might have the link text "Download our new brochure (PDF)". This can be important for assistive devices that can't read non-HTML files.

12 If you're linking to an email address so that people can contact you, make sure it's obvious that the link goes to an email address. It can be disorientating if visitors expect a link to open a new web page and find it opens their email program instead.

13 Don't open pages in a new window without warning the user. Users are often confused by new windows. Sometimes they don't notice them, so think the link hasn't worked. Other times, they get stuck in that window because they can't use the back button to return.

14 Don't have links that only show up or make sense when the mouse hovers over them, such as icons with explanatory text that only appears when the mouse rolls over them. It should be immediately obvious what a link does. Many devices (including touchscreen devices) can't simulate the mouse hovering, so their users can't make sense of those links.

6 HTML: The language of the web

Every web page is built using HTML, a special language for describing web content. In this chapter, you'll learn how it works, will be introduced to the most important tags, and will learn the principles of good HTML

What is HTML?

HTML is the language of the Internet. It's short for hypertext markup language, but don't let the jargon scare you off.

"Hypertext" is simply content that you navigate through using links, and "marking up" just means labeling the content so that the browser knows what to do with it.

A web page is basically a plain text file, which can only contain keyboard characters. It can't have bold or italic formatting embedded in it, like a Word document can.

The browser ignores white space in an HTML file, too, so it doesn't even know where the paragraph breaks are. HTML helps by adding instructions that explain to the browser how it should treat different parts of the page.

You create an HTML document by writing the text you want on your web page, and then adding *tags*. These are special pieces of code that use pointed brackets, which you might know better as greater than/less than signs. A < bracket is used to start a tag and a > is used to end it. Tags often come in pairs, so that they can mark the start and the end of text that should be treated in a particular way.

Here's some example HTML code:

```
<h1>This is the headline for the page</h1>
<p>Between the p tags, you find a paragraph.</p>
```

While the tags themselves might seem foreign, the idea is simple. The <h1> tag tells the browser that this is the most important headline on the page. The </h1> tag is used to mark the end of the headline.

The <p> and </p> tags are used to mark the start and end of the paragraph. When tags come in pairs, the second one uses a / to show it is a closing tag and not the start of the next tag.

You can create an HTML document using any text editor or word processor, such as Notepad or WordPad in Windows. Make sure you save as a text-only file, though, otherwise your file might include layout codes that the browser can't understand.

You can view the HTML for any web page on the Internet. In your browser, right-click on the web page and select View Source.

Hot tip

HTML filenames usually end with .htm or .html. Use only lower-case characters and numbers in your filenames, and don't include any spaces. Instead, use a hyphen to separate words. The homepage on a website is usually called index.htm or index.html.

Hot tip

To test an HTML file on your computer, open it in your web browser. In Internet Explorer or Chrome, use CTRL+O.

Structuring HTML pages

Although the content of web pages can be wildly different, the basic document structure is the same. You can see the code for a simple web page I've made here:

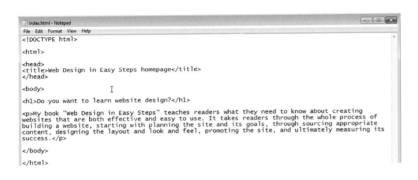

```
index.html - Notepad
File  Edit  Format  View  Help
<!DOCTYPE html>

<html>

<head>
<title>Web Design in Easy Steps homepage</title>
</head>

<body>            I

<h1>Do you want to learn website design?</h1>

<p>My book "Web Design in Easy Steps" teaches readers what they need to know about creating
websites that are both effective and easy to use. It takes readers through the whole process of
building a website, starting with planning the site and its goals, through sourcing appropriate
content, designing the layout and look and feel, promoting the site, and ultimately measuring its
success.</p>

</body>

</html>
```

This is what the different parts mean:

- The DOCTYPE tells the browser what version of HTML the web page is using. The doctype in my example is for HTML5, and most other doctypes are much longer and more complex. Browsers rarely use it, but it should be there anyway.

- The <html> and </html> tags mark the start and the end of the HTML document. Apart from the doctype, they're the first and last tags in the document.

- The <head> and </head> tags mark the header for the document. The header is used for things like search engine information (see Chapter 15) and linking to style sheets, which are used for layout and design (see Chapter 7).

- The <title> and </title> tags go in the header and are used for the page title. This is the name of the browser window when someone is viewing your page, the name of the bookmark if you add the page to your browser favorites, and is used in search engine results when Google suggests your web page.

- The <body> and </body> tags indicate where the web page content is. This is where you put the HTML code for what will appear on screen.

- You've already met the <h1> tag, but note that the on-screen headline doesn't have to be the same as the <title> tag.

Don't forget

You don't need fancy tools to create HTML. I've used Notepad here. It's a free part of Windows. You'll find it in the Accessories folder.

Hot tip

Because HTML5 is compatible with older versions of HTML, too, you can use this simple doctype, even on older web pages.

Adding pictures

To add a picture to your web page, use the <img> tag. You need to include four pieces of information, known as attributes:

- The *image source.* If your image file is in the same folder as the HTML file, then the image source will simply be its filename. Otherwise, you'll need to say which folder it's in, too. You can include images on different websites by adding the domain name and full path to the file, but you should get permission from that website first.

- The *width* and the *height* of the image in pixels. Including this helps the browser to speed up its display of the web page, because it knows how much space to set aside for pictures. If your image looks distorted, check the width and height attributes in your <img> tag. The browser displays your image at the size you specify, even if the image is a different shape.

- *Alternative text* for people who can't see the image. They might be people using a screenreader or someone who has switched images off because they have a poor connection. The alternative text should not contain additional or different information to the image. (You'll hear people call it an alt tag, but it's not, strictly speaking, a tag. It's the alt attribute.)

Here is an example <img> tag:

```
<img src="dog.jpg" width="250" height="150" alt="My
dog gnawing a bone">
```

This adds an image called dog.jpg into the web page with a width of 250 pixels and a height of 150 pixels. If the picture was in a folder called photos on a website called **www.example.com**, you would change the src to "**http://www.example.com/photos/dog.jpg**".

All the other tags we've seen so far enclose a piece of text, with an opening and closing tag marking the start and the end of the content they apply to. The <img> tag is different because it doesn't apply to a piece of text, so it doesn't have a closing tag. One version of HTML (called XHTML) required every tag to have a closing tag, though. To meet that requirement, people put a closing slash inside the IMG tag before its closing bracket. You don't need to do this, but you might see it in other web pages:

```
<img src="dog.jpg" width="250" height="150" alt="My
dog gnawing a bone" />
```

Don't forget

There are lots of different file types for images, but only JPG and GIF files are well supported by all web browsers. The GIF format supports transparency and simple animation. JPGs offer the best compression for photos.

Don't forget

Take care with the size of your images. Before putting them on your website, resize and compress them.

Adding links

What makes the web so effective is the ability to link from anywhere in any document to any other website or web page, anywhere on the web.

To add a link in HTML, use an anchor tag, like this:

```
<a href="booking.html">Book your ticket now!</a>
```

The href attribute tells the browser where the link goes, and the text between the anchor tags becomes the link text displayed on screen. When a website visitor clicks on that text, they will be taken to the booking.html page, which is in the same folder as the page they are currently reading.

To go up a level and link to a file in the folder above the current one use ../ at the start of the path. For example, if you need to reference the file dog.jpg that is above the current folder in the hierarchy, use: ../dog.jpg

To link to a picture in a folder called photos, which is on the same level as the current folder, go up a level, then down again: ../photos/dog.jpg

Adding external links
You can also link to another website, or a specific page on it. To link to Google, for example, you would use:

```
<a href="http://www.google.com">Visit Google</a>
```

You can use an image as a link instead of text, by replacing the link display text with an image tag, like this:

```
<a href="booking.html"><img src="bookingbutton.gif"
width="150" height="50" alt="Book now!"></a>
```

This technique is used on lots of websites to make clickable navigation buttons, or to make product pictures link to further information about the products.

Adding email links
You can also link to an email address. When the link is clicked, it will open a new email in the default email program. Make it obvious that the link is to an email address and not another web page. Here's some example code:

```
<a href="mailto:sean@example.com">Email me</a>
```

When linking to other people's websites, the page reference you use as the href attribute in your anchor tag is the same as what you see in the address bar of your browser, when you visit the web page.

87

If you're linking to another website, don't forget the "http://" in the link destination. If you just link to "www.google.com", it won't work.

Creating tables

HTML includes tags to enable you to lay out tabular information, such as a timetable or anything else that you might easily describe in a spreadsheet. The following picture shows how Wikipedia uses a table to communicate the capital city, size, and population for Germany's 16 states.

You could put an image tag inside a table cell, so you could include the state flag, for example. You can add links for more information, too, or any other HTML code.

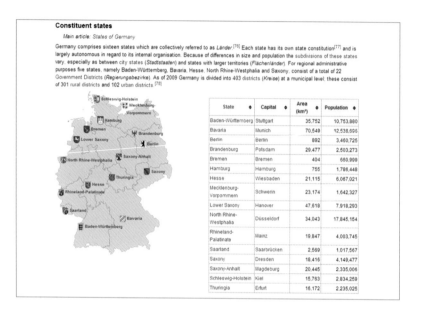

Constituent states

Main article: States of Germany

Germany comprises sixteen states which are collectively referred to as *Länder*.[76] Each state has its own state constitution[77] and is largely autonomous in regard to its internal organisation. Because of differences in size and population the subdivisions of these states vary, especially as between city states (*Stadtstaaten*) and states with larger territories (*Flächenländer*). For regional administrative purposes five states, namely Baden-Württemberg, Bavaria, Hesse, North Rhine-Westphalia and Saxony, consist of a total of 22 Government Districts (*Regierungsbezirke*). As of 2009 Germany is divided into 403 districts (*Kreise*) at a municipal level; these consist of 301 rural districts and 102 urban districts.[78]

State	Capital	Area (km²)	Population
Baden-Württemberg	Stuttgart	35,752	10,753,880
Bavaria	Munich	70,549	12,538,696
Berlin	Berlin	892	3,460,725
Brandenburg	Potsdam	29,477	2,503,273
Bremen	Bremen	404	660,999
Hamburg	Hamburg	755	1,786,448
Hesse	Wiesbaden	21,115	6,067,021
Mecklenburg-Vorpommern	Schwerin	23,174	1,642,327
Lower Saxony	Hanover	47,618	7,918,293
North Rhine-Westphalia	Düsseldorf	34,043	17,845,154
Rhineland-Palatinate	Mainz	19,847	4,003,745
Saarland	Saarbrücken	2,569	1,017,567
Saxony	Dresden	18,416	4,149,477
Saxony-Anhalt	Magdeburg	20,446	2,335,006
Schleswig-Holstein	Kiel	15,763	2,834,259
Thuringia	Erfurt	16,172	2,235,025

Marking up a table

The HTML code for tables can look complex because you have to indicate the start and end of the table, each row and each cell, resulting in a lot of HTML in a small space. But the tags are fairly intuitive:

- `<table>` and `</table>` mark the start and end of the table.

- `<caption>` and `</caption>` encapsulate a title for the table that summarizes its content. Unlike the summary, the caption appears on screen.

- `<tr>` and `</tr>` go around each table row.

- `<th>` and `<th>` go around each table heading cell. You can have a heading on a column or at the start of a row.

- `<td>` and `</td>` go around each table data item (which means each box on the table).

Remember to include closing tags. Old browsers can struggle to display the page if you forget to close your `<table>` tag with a `</table>` tag.

...cont'd

You can see the markup for a simple table of population values below. I've kept the table to three rows and four columns to avoid overcomplicating it. The first row is made up of headers for the columns. The next row starts with a header to say which state that row refers to, and then includes the different data items.

The top left cell of a table could be a header for its row or column. That's why its <th> tag includes a scope attribute, to explain that it's describing the content below it. This doesn't change what's on screen, but it helps with accessibility.

```
tables-example.htm - Notepad
File  Edit  Format  View  Help
<table>

<caption>Population of the United
States by State</caption>

<tr>
<th scope="col">State</th>
<th>Population</th>
<th>Density</th>
<th>Ranking by population</th>
</tr>

<tr>
<th>California</th>
<td>36.9 million</td>
<td>90.49/km2</td>
<td>1st</td>
</tr>

<tr>
<th>Nevada</th>
<td>2.6 million</td>
<td>9.02/km2</td>
<td>7th</td>
</tr>

<tr>
<th>Minnesota</th>
<td>5.2 million</td>
<td>25.21/km2</td>
<td>21st</td>
</tr>

</table>
```

This is what that table looks like in a browser:

Population of the United States by State

State	Population	Density	Ranking by population
California	36.9 million	90.49/km2	1st
Nevada	2.6 million	9.02/km2	7th
Minnesota	5.2 million	25.21/km2	21st

The headings, such as "Population" and "Density", are wrapped in <th> tags and appear bold on screen by default. I've added the border to the table for clarity here. You'll learn how to improve the presentation of your HTML in the next chapter.

So blind visitors don't have to remember too much, the screenreader can read the appropriate table heading before a data item. That's why I've made the state name a heading for each row: as well as being a data item, it provides useful context for the rest of the row.

Column1	Column2	Column3	Column4
Cell data	Cell data	Cell data	Cell data
rowspan="2"	Cell data	Cell data	Cell data
	Cell data	colspan="2"	
Cell data	Cell data	Cell data	Cell data

An example table, showing the effect of using rowspan and colspan.

Keep an eye on how big your table is. There's no technical limitation, but big tables are hard to use. If people have to trace their finger across the screen or scroll it to read your table, it's far too big.

More advanced tables

Creating cells that span multiple cells
Sometimes, you might want table cells to be different sizes. You might want one cell to have the same height as two cells to the right of it, or you might want one cell to stretch across two columns underneath it, for example. You can modify the <td> (or <th>) tag with a rowspan or colspan attribute to achieve this:

```
<td rowspan="2">This cell is as deep as two cells
</td>
```

When you use this markup, the cell stretches to occupy the space of the cell underneath it, too, so you will need one fewer cell on the next row. If you set the column span to 2, it will stretch to occupy the cell to its right as well, so you will need one fewer cell in the same row. You can have a colspan or rowspan of any value, so you can represent complex data.

Using tables for layout
You can put any HTML inside a table cell, so tables can be useful for structuring page layout. The page in the screenshot below, for example, uses a table to lay out a set of thumbnail photos.

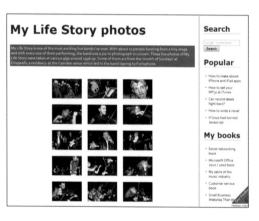

In the early days of the Internet, people used tables to lay out entire web pages. They would have one cell that spans two columns for the header, and then have two cells of different widths for the sidebar and the main content. Into these cells, they would then pour all their content and HTML markup. It was a clever workaround at a time when browsers had limited controls for laying out pages. But it resulted in slow and cumbersome pages.

Nowadays, you should use CSS for arranging your content on the screen, and limit your use of layout tables to small sections within the page that cannot be easily formatted another way.

What is a web form?

One basic way that visitors can interact with a website is by using a web form. The form analogy comes from paper forms, such as a credit card application form. A web form provides boxes where people can enter their information or select from options.

Below, you can see the form that Microsoft uses to gather your details when you register for a Microsoft account.

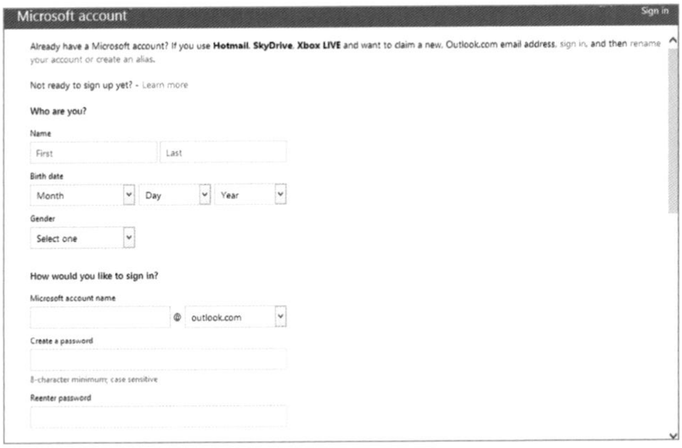

(Microsoft account registration form screenshot)

You could use a form on your website for any of the following:

- **A contact form.** Not as friendly for visitors as publishing an email address, but it means you can hide your email address from spammers. You can also prompt visitors with questions and give a box for each answer to encourage a response.

- **A search engine.** Make it easy for people to find what they need, by enabling them to type in some descriptive keywords, so you can find them all the pages that match.

- **An order form.** The easier it is for someone to buy from you, the more likely they are to do it. Enable them to enter their order requirements on your website, including delivery details and payment information.

HTML is used to structure the form, but you'll need a different technology to handle what the visitor enters into it. You might have a script (or program) on the server, for example, that returns search results or forwards their message to you by email, or you might use JavaScript to update the screen in response to the input.

(Google screenshot, top right)

How often do you use a web form? Several times a day, probably. A search engine is basically a tiny form. Google's has one text input box and two buttons.

Hot tip

Your hosting company probably provides you with a free form submission script, and this is by far the easiest way to get started with forms.

You can also find scripts online that are hosted on other people's servers. These will send your visitors' data to them first, and they will then make it available to you. If you use one of these scripts, make sure the provider is reputable.

Choosing form elements

There are several standard elements you can choose from to design a form in HTML. You've almost certainly used them all before when visiting other websites. They are:

- **A textbox**. This is used to accept a single line of text input, such as a name or an email address. It is possible to type more into a textbox than can be seen on screen at once, because the box scrolls. To make it easy to use, give it enough screen space so that people can see everything they are typing.

- **A textarea**. This is like a textbox, except that it enables you to enter multiple lines of information. You might use it to accept comments on a contact form. You could use a textarea to accept an address, but that information will be more useful and complete if you prompt people to enter each line (street address, town, state, etc.) into a different textbox. Only use a textarea where the format of the data doesn't really matter.

- **Radio buttons**. These are used to choose only one option from a group. If one button is selected, all the others are automatically de-selected. They might be used to ask for information, such as gender (male or female), where the answers are mutually exclusive. Radio buttons are round.

- **Checkboxes**. These enable people to choose options by ticking a box beside them. People can check multiple boxes, so they might be used to indicate a number of different interests. Checkboxes are square.

- **Select menus**. These save screen space by only opening up their options when clicked. They are harder to use than radio buttons or checkboxes, and should only be used for options that can be easily navigated when users can't see all the options at once. They're most often used to complete an address using an alphabetically sorted list of countries.

- **Buttons.** Every form needs a button that people can click to confirm they've finished completing it. It's often called a submit button, but it might actually say something else on it. For example, Google's button says "Google Search" and eBay's button for logging in says "Sign in". Pressing the Enter key should have the same effect as clicking the submit button.

Hot tip

It takes time to enter information into a website and users will be put off by a long and complicated form. Only ask for essential information. If you do need a long form, consider splitting the process over multiple short screens. It makes the process more approachable and also gives you a chance to follow up on incomplete submissions if you collect basic contact details first.

Beware

If you are going to ask people to enter personal and payment information into a form, make sure you have a secure server that encrypts the data as it crosses the Internet. Your hosting company can help with this.

Forms can look and behave differently in different browsers and on different devices.

The mobile version of Safari, used on the iPhone and iPod among other devices, has a more rounded look to the form controls than the Windows versions of Safari or Internet Explorer. The submit button is lozenge shaped instead of square, and textboxes and textareas have rounded corners. Checkboxes go from white to black when ticked, providing more contrast, too.

The select element operates completely differently in the mobile version of Safari. On a desktop, it opens a pulldown menu that the user can pick from (see above). On the iPod or iPhone, it opens a barrel roll slider that takes up half the screen. That makes it easier for users to choose using the touchscreen.

Don't try to enforce a standard form appearance across all devices. Your site will be easier to use if its form elements look the same as those people usually see on their device.

Form elements displayed in Internet Explorer

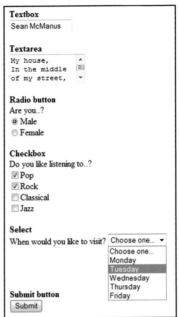

Sometimes forms have a reset button, but I don't recommend it. The risk of someone pressing it by mistake when they want to submit the form is far greater than the likelihood that someone will want to start over.

93

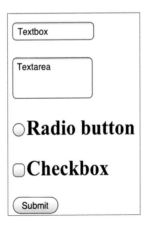

Left: Form elements, including the select element (right), displayed in Safari Mobile

Hot tip

You can change the size of a textbox on screen to 20 characters by adding size="20" to its tag. This only affects how much you can see at once, not how much can be entered into the box. To limit the text that can be entered to 20 characters, use maxlength="20".

Hot tip

Labels make form elements easier for everyone to use. You can click a label beside a textbox to put your cursor in it, and can click a label for a radio button or checkbox to select it. That means users don't have to be so precise in using the mouse.

Using the input tag

Here is a simple form that just asks somebody to enter their name. With just one data box, it's meaningless, but it shows how the form and input tags work together to create your form:

```
<form method="post" action="senddata.php">
<label for="lastname">Last name:</label>
<input type="text" id="lastname" name="lastname">
<input type="submit" value="Submit form!">
</form>
```

This is what it looks like on screen:

The <form> and </form> tags wrap the whole form. The action part of the tag tells the web browser where to send this data, in this case, to a script called senddata on the same server as the form itself. This form won't actually do anything when you submit if you don't have a script to process the form data.

A textbox is just a hole on the screen, so you need to add some text near it to explain what should be entered into it. So that screenreaders know which explanation belongs to which form element, you wrap <label> and </label> tags around it. You specify which form element the label belongs to by making the "for" attribute in the label the same as the id attribute in the input tag. Designers typically position labels on screen above or to the left of the form element for text fields and to the right of radio buttons or checkboxes.

The input tag itself has several attributes. The type is used to specify which element it is, in this case a textbox. The id is used to uniquely identify the element so it can be associated with a label or so that CSS can be used to change its appearance later.

To help you untangle the data when it comes through to your script, the name attribute is submitted along with the form data.

To avoid confusion when you're building the site, the name can be the same as the id attribute, as it is here, but it doesn't have to be.

The table below outlines the other input types you can use. To add a set of radio buttons for gender, for example, with the labels to the right of them, insert the following code. It can go anywhere between the <form> and </form> tags:

```
<input type="radio" value="male"
id="male" name="gender">
<label for="male">Male</label>
<br>
<input type="radio" value="female"
id="female" name="gender">
<label for="female">Female</label>
```

If you want to make a particular radio button or checkbox selected by default, put the word "checked" (without quotes) before the closing bracket of its input tag. The value attribute defines what data will be sent to the server when the form is submitted.

The iPad uses the new HTML5 input types to make it easier to input information: it shows you a different keyboard depending on what you're entering. The email keyboard displays when the input type is email and has a prominent @ sign, while the telephone keyboard uses large numbers like a calculator. You can start using these types now and they will default to a textbox where they are not supported.

Hot tip

If you want to make a text box compulsory, put the word "required" before its closing bracket. This is an HTML5 feature that is not yet supported on all browsers.

Hot tip

The <br> tag adds a line break.

Form element	Input type	Notes
textbox	text	See example on facing page.
radio button	radio	All radio buttons with the same name attribute belong to the same group, only one of which can be selected.
checkbox	checkbox	Each checkbox should have a unique name attribute.
submit button	submit	The value attribute defines the text that will appear on the button.
reset button (clear form)	reset	The value attribute defines the text that will appear on the button.
password box	password	This functions the same as a textbox, except that what is typed in is not shown on screen. Dots are used to show the number of characters typed.
email address box	email	New for HTML5. Older browsers default to a textbox.
website address box	url	New for HTML5. Older browsers default to a textbox.
phone number box	tel	New for HTML5. Older browsers default to a textbox.
date box	date	New for HTML5. Older browsers default to a textbox.

If you put text between the <textarea> and </textarea> tags, this will be the default text in the textbox.

Don't forget to enclose your whole form in <form> and </form> tags.

Using other form elements

The input tag is used to create nearly all form elements, but there are two more form elements that use their own tags.

Creating a multiline text box

A textbox with multiple lines is created using the tag <textarea>. The cols attribute gives the width on screen in characters and the rows attribute is the height of the box in lines of text. Users can enter more information and the box will scroll to accommodate it. Note that a closing </textarea> tag is required, even if there's nothing between the tags as in this case. Here's some example markup:

```
<label for="comments">Your feedback:</label>
<textarea id="comments" name="comments" cols="20"
rows="5">
</textarea>
```

Creating select menus

To create a select menu, you use a combination of two new tags. The <select> and </select> tags go at the start and the end of the menu. Within them, you put your options, each one marked up with an <option> and </option> tag.

The value attribute on the <option> tag defines what will be submitted if that particular option is selected. It doesn't have to be the same as what is presented to the user. In my example below, the user might select "Alabama" on screen, but the server will be sent the code of "AL".

```
<label for="state">State:</label><select id="state"
name="state">
<option value="--" selected>Choose one...</option>
<option value="AL">Alabama</option>
<option value="AK">Alaska</option>
<option value="AZ">Arizona</option>
<!-- other state options go here -->
</select>
```

To set the default value for a select menu, add the word "selected" to its <option> tag, as I have here for the first option.

People who don't choose anything might have their preference indicated as the first item in your list when the form is submitted. By adding a "Choose one..." option and making it the default item, you can easily see when this has happened.

Creating lists

Sometimes all you need are simple bullet points to get your message across.

HTML includes tags for marking up bulleted lists (known as unordered lists) and numbered lists (known as ordered lists). You can change the format of the numbers or bullets using CSS.

You can also use a list to mark up the links in a navigation bar, and then use CSS to change the default layout so the items are displayed side by side on screen, but can be easily navigated as a list when using devices like screenreaders.

To create a list, start with a <ul> or <ol> tag for an unordered or ordered list. Then put a <li> tag before each list item. You can optionally use a closing tag of </li> at the end of each item, if you want to.

Here's an HTML paragraph that includes a numbered list:

```
There are 5 Die Hard films:
<ol>
<li>Die Hard
<li>Die Hard 2: Die Harder
<li>Die Hard With a Vengeance
<li>Live Free or Die Hard
<li>A Good Day to Die Hard
</ol>
These all star Bruce Willis.
```

The screenshot below shows what it looks like on screen. Note that, by default, each list item starts on a new line, and that the text after the list starts a new block of text on screen, even without a new paragraph tag.

Beware

If you forget your closing </ol> or </ul> tag, the rest of your web page's paragraphs might be indented on screen.

There are 5 Die Hard films:

1. Die Hard
2. Die Hard 2: Die Harder
3. Die Hard With a Vengeance
4. Live Free or Die Hard
5. A Good Day to Die Hard

These all star Bruce Willis.

The art of good HTML

The purpose of HTML has changed over the years. In the early days of the commercial web, HTML was used to lay out a web page and format it visually. It included a mix of the content and the design. Now, as you will see in Chapter 7, we use CSS for formatting, and HTML should be used primarily for marking up the structure of your content.

That means your HTML should be adding meaning to your content, and should be reasonably independent of the on-screen appearance. If you're dictating the design of your web page in HTML, you're doing it wrong!

Choosing the right tags to mark up your content

You've already seen how the <h1> tag can be used to indicate the most important headline on a page. There are also tags for <h2>, <h3> and all the way down to <h6>. In practice, people rarely use headings deeper than <h3>.

The headings will (by default) be different sizes on screen, with the <h1> heading being the largest. You can't just use <h1> to make text big and <h6> to make it small, though: you have to use the heading tags for headlines, otherwise your HTML doesn't make sense. Remember that your HTML won't always be used on a PC screen: sometimes screenreaders will use your markup to navigate between sections of the page, and sometimes search engines will use it to work out what's important when indexing your site.

Similarly, the <strong> tag will usually make text bold. Its proper use, though, is not to change what text looks like, but to indicate text that has strong importance. The <em> tag for emphasis typically shows italicised text, but should be used only for text that you would emphasise when reading it out. If you use tags like these to mark up large areas to text, just to change their appearance in your browser, you make the web page potentially meaningless, or at least hard to use, for other devices.

Ask yourself whether the markup you're adding helps people to navigate your content using any device, or whether it is specific to what the web page looks like on your PC screen.

If it's specific to a PC screen, consider whether you can use CSS to achieve the same effect instead.

Don't forget

To make your document logical, you have to use the heading tags in order, so that a <h3> heading can only appear inside a section titled with a <h2>, which is, itself, inside a section titled with a <h1>.

This is heading 1

This is heading 2

This is heading 3

This is heading 4

This is heading 5

This is heading 6

Headings 1 to 6, as seen in Internet Explorer.

Keep accessibility in mind

It's easy to do the wrong thing with HTML. You could fake table headers using fancy formatting, or omit labels from your forms. If you feed sloppy HTML into a browser, it won't warn you. It'll just do its best with whatever you throw at it. But if you don't mark up tables or forms correctly, they may become unusable by those who depend on assistive devices. The more accessible your HTML is, the more likely it is to work on devices you haven't tested and on new browsers that are released.

Commenting your code

The examples in this chapter are trivial, but a real web page can be extremely complicated. When you come back to modify a page later, it can be hard to understand the markup. To avoid confusion, add comments to your HTML by putting <!-- at the start and --> at the end of the comment like this:

```
</div> <!-- Closes wrapper div -->
```

These comments are not presented to the site visitor but can be seen if anybody views your source. Add comments to help you remember why you coded something the way you did.

The finished HTML

Your finished HTML web page will look pretty unremarkable, as you can see in my example below. All the content will be in a single column that fills the page width, and all the text will be black. But the content should look like it's structured logically. In the next chapter, you will learn how to change the layout and appearance of your web page.

Avoid using the <font> and <frame> tags, and the align, border and color attributes on tags. These are deprecated, which means they're officially out-of-date. Future browsers might not support them.

Even when your website is in its early stages, you can ask people to test it and give you feedback. It's best to test your website early and often, so that you can refine the design throughout, and don't incur a lot of rework at the end.

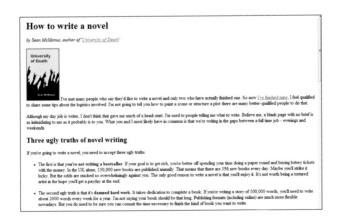

If you just want to mark up a few words in the middle of a sentence, you put <span> and </span> tags around them. Think first, though, whether you would be better off using <em> or <strong> tags to indicate emphasis or something of greater importance. The <span> tag doesn't mean anything, but those other tags do.

When you use a </div>, it always closes the most recent <div> that is still open.

Right: How <div> sections of a web page might be named and laid out.

Dividing the page up

Using CSS (see Chapter 7), you can change the appearance and location of different sections of HTML content. So how do you mark where a section begins and ends?

Designers often use <div> and </div> tags to indicate the start and end of each section. You might have a section for navigation, the main article content of the page, a sidebar, and the page footer, for example. Each section would probably include a mixture of content and HTML tags.

You can put sections inside sections if you need to. If you look at a magazine, you might notice they often use a large quote from an interview in the middle of an article, to break it up and draw you in. To do that on a web page, you might use <div> tags to create a pullquote section inside the <div> tags for your article.

The sections often correspond closely with the different boxes of content on the screen, which is a handy rule of thumb. You might put all your sections inside a wrapper or container section, so that you can put a single border around everything, or put all your content in a colored box that is centered on the page.

So that you can change a section's appearance later, you need to be able to identify each section. To do that, you add a class attribute to each <div> tag. "Class" just means "type", so, if you give a <div> a class of "pullquote", it means that section is a pullquote section. It doesn't necessarily mean that it's the only pullquote section. You can reuse the same class, so you can apply the same design to all your pullquotes, for example.

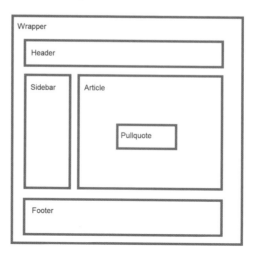

...cont'd

The following code shows how the typical web page might be organized using <div> sections.

```
<div class="wrapper">
<div class="header"> Header HTML here </div>
<div class="sidebar"> Sidebar HTML here </div>
<div class="article"> Article starts here
<div class="pullquote"> Pullquote here </div>
Article ends here. </div>
<div class="footer"> Footer content here </div>
</div>
```

Note how the pullquote is inside the article section, because it is defined before the article <div> is closed. All the sections are inside the wrapper section, because it's opened at the start of the page and closed at the end, with all the other sections inside it.

What's new in HTML5?

HTML5 introduces some standard tags that you can use to mark up different parts of your web page instead of using <div> sections. These new tags are <section>, used to mark up thematically linked content; <header>, which is used for introductory or navigational aids; <footer>, which is used to provide more information, such as copyright information; <aside>, which is used for loosely related information, such as a pullquote; <nav>, which is used for a significant group of navigation links; and <article>, which is used for an article. Each one is closed using a close tag, such as </nav> or </aside>.

These new tags enable more meaningful HTML, so that browsers and search engines can help users navigate your content easily. The tags raise some tricky questions, though. You can have an article inside a section or a section inside an article, for example. Choose your tags with care to ensure they make sense.

Here's that same web page template with the <div> tags replaced with HTML5 tags where they make sense:

```
<div class="wrapper">
<header> Header HTML here </header>
<aside> Sidebar HTML here </aside>
<article> Article starts here
<div class="pullquote"> Pullquote here </div>
Article ends here. </article>
<footer> Footer content here </footer>
</div>
```

This HTML doesn't do anything to change the presentation of your article by itself. You'll need to use CSS to actually create the boxes.

Versions of Internet Explorer that predate HTML5 don't handle these well, so you need to add some code to make them compatible. See **http://code.google.com/p/html5shiv**

Beware

Many (perhaps most) HTML tutorials online were written some years ago, and might recommend outdated techniques (such as frames) and tags (such as <font>). The web is a great source of information, but make sure what you're reading is current. To get further up-to-date HTML techniques visit **www.ineasysteps.com** for the latest edition of **HTML in easy steps**.

Hot tip

Serverside includes enable you to share chunks of HTML between different web pages. You could share the header, so you only have one file to update when you add new links to the navbar, for example. There isn't room to cover this technology here, but you can find tutorials online, including on my website.

Your next steps with HTML

If you plan to publish any content online, a working knowledge of HTML is a great asset. It's useful whether you intend to build your own website, need to include HTML markup in your blog posts, or just want to add some formatting to your comments on somebody else's blog.

This chapter provides a whirlwind tour through the most common tags and concepts and has hopefully whetted your appetite to learn more.

The most authoritative source of information on HTML tags, and how they should be used, is the W3C website at **www.w3.org** The World Wide Web Consortium (W3C for short) develops the HTML standards and publishes them in full on its website, including those that are still in development. They can be rather dry reading and are written very much in the style of a computer manual, so it takes some time to get used to their style and jargon. At the top of each specification is a link to the latest version of it.

There are many books dedicated to HTML that go into greater depth, such as HTML5 in easy steps, than this chapter and provide more examples, and you can find lots of examples online.

You can check how well your HTML adheres to the HTML standards using a validator. The one at **http://validator.w3.org** will take a web page or uploaded file and highlight any errors on it. It's best practice to try to write code that validates. The validator identifies errors such as missing or duplicate closing tags, so you can clean up your code.

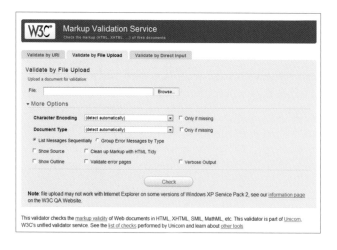

Reference: structure

HTML tag	Description
`<!DOCTYPE html>`	Defines the version of HTML being used. This simple doctype is for HTML5.
`<html>...` `<html>`	Used to indicate the start and end of the HTML document.
`<head>...` `</head>`	Used to define the boundaries of the header of the document, where meta tags, scripts and CSS links go.
`<title>...` `</title>`	Used to mark the title of the web page, which will be its link text in search engine listings and its default bookmark title. The title goes inside the header.
`<body>...` `</body>`	Used to define the boundaries of the body of the document, where the marked-up content is.
`<div class="classname">` `...` `</div>`	Used to mark the start and end of a section of content. A <div> section can enclose large chunks of content and markup, including one or more paragraphs. See Chapter 7.
`<span class="classname">` `...` `</span>`	Marks the start and end of a piece of content (within a paragraph or heading) and gives it a particular class name. See Chapter 7.
`<header>...</header>`	Used for introductory or navigational aids.
`<footer>...</footer>`	Used for additional information, such as copyright details.
`<nav>...</nav>`	Used for a significant group of navigation links or a navbar.
`<article>...</article>`	Marks the start and end of an article.
`<section>...</section>`	Indicates the start and end of a logical content section.
`<aside> ... </aside>`	Indicates loosely related content, such as a pullquote.

You can add a comment to your HTML to help you remember how your web page works. The browser ignores comments. By surrounding a chunk of HTML with comment symbols, you can hide it from the browser and switch it off. This is what a comment looks like:

`<!-- comment -->`

The tags <header>, <footer>, <nav>, <article>, <section>, and <aside> were introduced in HTML5, the latest version of the HTML standard. You'll need to add a workaround to make them work in older versions of IE. See the CSS Chapter for more information.

The meta tags, style sheet link, and favorites icons links go between your <head> and </head> tags.

Above: some examples of home screen icons for websites.

Reference: header

Meta tags
Meta tags feed additional information to search engines (see Chapter 15):

```
<meta name="Description" content="Description goes here">
<meta name="Keywords" content="keyword1, keyword2, keyword3...">
```

Adding a style sheet
See Chapter 7 for an explanation of style sheets. To add an external style sheet for the screen, use this line:

```
<link href="folder/filename.css" rel="stylesheet" type="text/css" media="screen">
```

Adding an external JavaScript file
JavaScript (see Chapter 8) often needs to be added between the <head> and </head> tags (depending on what the script does), but it can go anywhere in your web page (depending on the script). The page will often load faster if it's put just before the </body> tag. To add a JavaScript file to your web page, use this line:

```
<script src="filename.js" type="text/javascript"></script>
```

Adding favorites icons
You can add an icon to your web page, called a favicon, which appears in bookmarks and in the address bar in IE. It should be a 32 x 32 pixel .ico format image file. You can make one using the free program Irfanview (**www.irfanview.com**). If it is in the root (the same place as your homepage HTML file) and called favicon.ico, you don't need any code. If it isn't, or if you want different favicons for different pages, use this snippet of HTML:

```
<link href="favicon.ico" rel="shortcut icon">
```

You can also provide an icon that will be used if someone adds a web page to their iPhone, iPod or iPad home screen. It should be 152 x 152 pixels and square. If it is in the root and called apple-touch-icon.png, you don't need any code. If it isn't, or if you want different icons for different pages, use this:

```
<link rel="apple-touch-icon" href="customIcon.png">
```

Reference: text and forms

Content formatting

HTML tag	Description

`<h1> ... </h1>`
`<h2> ... </h2>`
`<h3> ... </h3>`
	Used to mark up headings. `<h1>` is the most important heading. Headings go down to `<h6>`.

`<p> ... </p>`	Used to mark the start and end of a paragraph.
`<strong> ...` `</strong>`	Important content, shown by default in bold on screen.
`<em> ... </em>`	Emphasized content, italicized by default.
`<blockquote> ...` `</blockquote>`	Used to mark up a paragraph-length quote (or longer), or an excerpt from another website.
` `	Line break.
`<hr>`	Horizontal line.

Hot tip

You can find the full HTML specification at **www.w3.org** Anything in HTML4 is pretty well supported by most browsers in use. HTML5, the latest version of HTML, is not fully implemented by all browsers. Use it, but be aware of how your web page will work for someone using an incompatible or old browser.

Forms

HTML tag	Description
`<form> ... </form>`	Marks the start and end of a form.
`<label for="id">Label text</label>`	Identifies the label for the form element with a given ID.
`<input type="textbox" id="id" name="name" size="20">`	A one-line textbox that accepts 20 characters. The size is optional. Alternative input types which cannot take a size are radio, checkboxw, submit, and reset. New text input types in HTML5 are password, email, url, tel and date.
`<textarea id="id" name="name" cols="20" rows="5">Default text in the box</textarea>`	A multiline text input box with 20 columns and 5 rows. Anything between these tags becomes the default text in the box.
`<select id="id" name="name"> ... </select>`	Marks the start and end of a select menu. Options go between the tags.
`<option value="value">Option text</option>`	Marks up each option in a select menu.

Hot tip

There are special codes to insert symbols. Use `&copy;` for a copyright sign, ` ` for a non-breaking space (one between two words that you don't want to be on different lines), `&amp;` for ampersand, `&lt;` and `&gt;` for < and >, and `&quot;` for speech marks. There are also codes for accented letters. Don't forget the semicolon.

Tables, lists, links, images

HTML tag	Description
`<table>` ... `</table>`	Marks the start and end of a table.
`<caption>` ... `</caption>`	Used to indicate a caption for the table which will appear on screen, unlike its summary.
`<th>` ... `</th>`	Marks the start and end of the header cell for a row or column. If it's ambiguous, indicate whether it is a header for a row or column by adding a scope to the opening tag: `<th scope="col">` or `<th scope="row">`
`<tr>` ... `</tr>`	Marks the start and end of a table row.
`<td>` ... `</td>`	Marks a table cell. To make the cell span across multiple rows or columns, add a rowspan and/or colspan element to the opening tag: `<td rowspan="2">` or `<td colspan="4">`

Bulleted and numbered lists

HTML tag	Description
`<ul>` ... `</ul>`	Defines the start and end of an unordered (bulleted) list.
`<ol>` ... `</ol>`	Defines the start and end of an ordered (numbered) list.
`<li>`	Marks the start of a list item. You can use `</li>` to close a list item, but that is usually unnecessary because the next element is another list item or the end of the list.

Don't forget

These tags enable you to create sophisticated documents, but this chapter is just a short summary of the most often used HTML tags.

Links: Example HTML

```
<a href="linkdestination">Link text or image here</a>
```

Link destination can be a filename on the current site (eg index. html) or a full URL (e.g. **http://www.example.com/aboutus.html**).

Images: Example HTML

```
<img src="filename.jpg" width="250" height="150" alt="alternative text description here">
```

7 CSS: Giving your pages some style

CSS is used to style what your web pages look like, including colors, fonts, and layout. In this chapter, you will learn how to create a simple page layout, how to build a navbar and how to make a print style sheet. You'll also pick up the skills you need to experiment with your own CSS web page designs and layouts.

Why use CSS?

As you saw last chapter, HTML can be used to mark up the structure of your document, but plain HTML looks rather uninspiring. To change the appearance and layout of your document, you use a technique called CSS.

CSS is short for cascading style sheets. The idea is that you put all the instructions for the design of your web page into a separate document called a style sheet. That single style sheet can be shared by lots of different web pages.

It is possible to put style instructions into your HTML file, but it's better to separate your content and design for several reasons:

● When it's time to refresh your site's look, you won't have to trawl through all your HTML files – just update your style sheet and the design across your whole site will change.

● It's easier to edit your HTML page content, too, because it's not cluttered up with layout and design instructions.

● You can easily define style sheets for different media (such as print and screen). This means you can use the same HTML to deliver web pages that are optimized for different devices.

● Removing the style from your HTML pages makes them smaller, and the style sheet can be cached for use across your site. That means the site will download more quickly because visitors won't need to download the same layout instructions in different web pages.

● Your design is more likely to degrade gracefully if you use style sheets and structural HTML. It might not look great on an ancient browser, but it should still work okay.

● Users can specify their own style sheet to use on your page (in IE, go to Tools/Options/Accessibility), so they can customize their experience of your site. This could be particularly valuable for those using assistive technology, such as screenreaders or Braille screens.

● Using style sheets makes it easier to enforce a consistent design across a whole web page and a whole website. You can ensure that all your headings look the same, for example, or that all your images have the same border on them.

Transforming your HTML

One way to appreciate the difference that CSS makes is to visit the CSS Zen Garden (**www.csszengarden.com**). This website provides a simple HTML file and invites designers to submit style sheets to improve its presentation. It's inspiring to see how many different designs can be created, without changing the HTML file. It shows you how radical a redesign you could make to your own website without even touching its HTML.

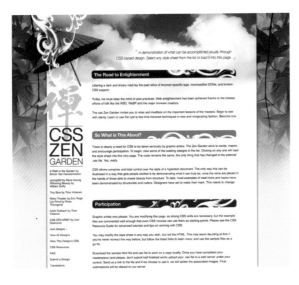

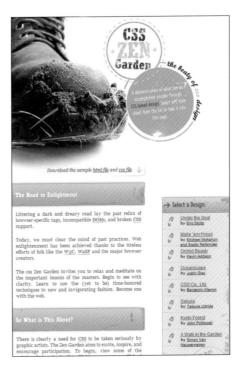

Three different CSS designs for the same HTML, from the CSS Zen Garden. Left: the Kyoto Forest design by John Politowski (**www.rpmdesignfactory.com**). Above: A Walk in the Garden by Simon Van Hauwermeiren. Top left: CSS Co Ltd by Benjamin Klemm.

Beware

The brackets you need are the curled brackets that look like an archery bow {like this}. It won't work if you use the rounded brackets used in written text (like this), or square brackets [like this].

Hot tip

If you're not American, note that CSS uses US spellings for color and center.

How CSS describes design

Each CSS statement has three elements to it:

- Information about which element of the web page you want to modify the appearance of. This is called the selector. For example, you might use one CSS statement to change all the <h2> headings, or a particular paragraph.

- The name of which detail of that element you want to change. This is called the property. That might be its text color, the border thickness, or the spacing between the element and others on the page.

- Finally, you need to tell the browser what to change that property to. For example, the color red, or a thickness of 4 pixels. We'll call this the value.

You can group CSS statements for the same selectors to save space, and to make it easier to understand what's going on. You can also assign the same style rules to as many selectors as you want at the same time. Here's what the CSS syntax might look like if you wanted to change two things about two selectors:

```
selector, selector {
property: value;
property: value;
}
```

As with HTML, you can space out your document however you want. Each rule has to end with a semi colon, so the browser knows when it's finished. If things don't work as expected, first check your semi colons are present and correct.

That looks a bit abstract, so here's a real example. What if you wanted to change your <h1> and <h2> headings so that they have red text and a red line underneath them, like the illustration below? Try this CSS:

```
h1, h2
{
color:red;
border-bottom:1px solid red;
}
```

First headline h1

Lorem ipsum dolor sit amet, consectetuer adipiscing elit. Maecenas porttitor congue massa. Fusce posuere, magna sed pulvinar ultricies.

Second headline h2

Proin pharetra nonummy pede. Mauris et orci. Aenean nec lorem. In porttitor. Donec laoreet nonummy augue.

Adding CSS to your site

The best way to use CSS is to put all your style instructions into a separate text file, called a style sheet. Like HTML documents, style sheets can be written using any text editor. They traditionally have the file extension .css. While you would have one HTML document for each web page on your site, you would only have a few style sheets shared across your site, perhaps only one.

The way that you link your HTML file to your CSS file is to add some code to your HTML document. Unfortunately, you do need to do this for each HTML page of your website. If you had a style sheet called main.css, for example, you would add this line of HTML between the <head> and </head> tags in your web pages:

```
<link href="main.css" rel="stylesheet" type="text/
css">
```

There are two other ways you can add style instructions to your website, but I don't recommend you use them often. Both of them make your site harder to manage, because you end up with design instructions spread across lots of different files.

Adding style instructions in the HTML document

The first is to add style instructions between the <head> tags of your HTML document. This might be useful if you had one page on your web site with a radically different design for some reason. You put <style> tags around your CSS statements, like this:

```
<head>
<style type="text/css">
h1 {color:red;}
h2 {color:blue;}
</style>
</head>
```

Adding style instructions to a HTML tag

You can also add style to a specific HTML tag, known as an inline style. You have to add it to every instance of every tag where you want it to take effect, though. You could use this to occasionally override a style sheet, but it's better to design the style sheet so you don't have to. Because you're adding the style to a tag, you don't need to provide a selector. Here's an example of how it works:

```
<h1 style="color:red;">First headline</h1>
```

I'm using code excerpts here. You'll probably have other things between your <head> tags, too, and that's okay. Just keep them outside your <style> tags.

If there's a conflict, the rule applies that is most specific to a particular element. For example, an inline style trumps styles in the header, which beat styles in an external style sheet. If a style mentions an element by its name, then that trumps any generic styles applied to all elements of that type.

It doesn't matter whether you use upper or lower case for your hexadecimal digits. I prefer upper case because all the symbols are more or less the same size. That can help you to spot errors, such as missing digits, more easily.

There is a shorthand you can use if the red, green, and blue values all use the same digit twice. You only need to use one of them. For example, #F0F is the same as #FF00FF and #369 is the same as #336699.

How to change colors

So far, I've been using the color "red". Red is one of just 16 colors that have a standard name in HTML and CSS. With such a small palette to choose from, designers rarely use the color names (except, perhaps, for red, black and white). Instead, they specify colors using a hexadecimal number.

What's hexadecimal?

We have ten fingers and toes, so our number system is based around the number ten (it's called base 10). Hexadecimal is the kind of counting system we might have if our species had evolved with 16 fingers and toes (base 16). Because we don't have enough number symbols, it uses the letters A to F as well as the digits 0 to 9. When you count in hexadecimal, it looks like this:

0, 1, 2, 3, 4, 5, 6, 7, 8, 9, A, B, C, D, E, F, 10, 11, 12 … 19, 1A, 1B, 1C, 1D, 1E, 1F, 20, 21, 22 … 29, 2A, 2B, 2C, 2D, 2E, 2F, 30, 31… 9D, 9E, 9F, A0, A1, A2 … AE, AF, B0, B1, B2…

It's similar to how we usually count. We keep counting until we've used up all the symbols (including A to F in hexadecimal), and then we increase the next column to the left by one. The numbers don't mean the same thing as they do in our regular number system, though. In our normal number system, 23 means two tens plus three. In hexadecimal, it means two sixteens plus three. The largest two-digit hexadecimal number you can have is FF (which is 255 in base 10).

You don't have to understand how to count in hexadecimal to create a website, but you do need some basic familiarity with it. It helps to understand whether one hexadecimal number is bigger than another. And now you know how the system works, you know that you can't have any letters apart from A-F in there, so it will be easier to spot mistakes.

Putting a zero on the front of the number doesn't change the meaning of that number. It does, however, make it easier for the browser to understand where one number ends and another begins. So if you want to use a number that's less than 10, you will usually add a zero to the front of it to make sure that it is still two digits.

For example:

00, 01, 02, 03, 04… 09, 0A, 0B, 0C, 0D, 0E, 0F

Describing colors with hexadecimal

Colors on web pages work a bit like mixing paints. To define a color, you tell the browser how much red, green, and blue you want to use, in that order. Each color is measured on a scale that goes from 00 to FF and they're all combined to create what looks like a single six-digit hexadecimal number, but is, in fact, three numbers glued together. A # sign is used in front of it.

So black, for example, is the absence of any color and so has the number #000000. A vivid red would have as much red as possible (FF), diluted by no green or blue, so it would be #FF0000. If you want to tone the default yellow color down a bit, you could add some blue and, instead of using #FFFF00, use #FFFFCC. Feel free to dabble with the colors.

Color	Hex	HTML name
	#000000	Black
	#C0C0C0	Silver
	#808080	Gray
	#FFFFFF	White
	#800000	Maroon
	#FF0000	Red
	#800080	Purple
	#FF00FF	Fuchsia
	#008000	Green
	#00FF00	Lime
	#808000	Olive
	#FFFF00	Yellow
	#000080	Navy
	#0000FF	Blue
	#008080	Teal
	#00FFFF	Aqua

Above: the 16 color names you can use in HTML, with their hex value equivalents

Hot tip

There is another way to specify colors, called RGBA. It uses base 10 numbers between 0 and 255 for red, green and blue. It adds a number between 0 and 1 for the level of opacity. For example: rgba(255,0,0,1) is solid red; rgba(0,0,255, 0.5) is semi-transparent blue. It can be used to enable some optional special effects on some browsers, but Internet Explorer didn't support it until IE9, so you can't rely on it.

113

Changing color

To color the text in an element, you change its color property. The element's background-color property can also be changed:

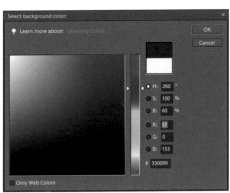

```
h1 {
color: #FFFFFF;
background-color:
#008080;
}
```

Don't forget

There are online tools to help you design color palettes, such as **www.colorscheme designer.com** If you create images on your PC, the color picker in Photoshop (or Photoshop Elements, shown on the left) gives you a hex value for any colors you choose, too.

Styling your text

Choosing fonts using CSS is easy. You just need to tell the browser which font-family you want to use.

If the font name has a space in it (such as Times New Roman), you put quotes around it. So this is how you set your <h2> headings to use Times New Roman:

```
h2 { font-family: "Times New Roman"; }
```

With so many different operating system versions and computer types out there, you can only use a tiny subset of the dozens of fonts on your computer with confidence. Because the browser uses the fonts on the visitor's computer to display your web page, you need to give the browser some choices. Tell it which font you want it to use first, but also give it some options for if that font isn't available.

Finally, if it doesn't have any of the named fonts you recommend, you can give it some generic font types to use.

Serif: abcdef
Sans-serif:abcdef

The most useful generic types are serif and sans-serif. Serifs are like little ticks of the pen at the end of the strokes on the letters. "Sans" just means without, so a sans-serif font doesn't have those details. Compare the letters S, r, i, b, and d on the left. There is also a monospace generic type, where each character takes up the same amount of space.

You list your font choices in order of preference, like this:

```
h2 { font-family: Calibri, Geneva, Arial, sans-serif;
}
```

Beware

Using the Comic Sans font is seen as a hallmark of amateur web design by professional web designers. The font has become overused, so it's better to choose something else.

Calibri was introduced for the first time in Windows Vista, so it won't be available on older Windows PCs. It doesn't ship with Mac OS, so it's unlikely to be supported on Apple computers. They will use the next preference Geneva font, though, which is well established on the Mac (but not on Windows). As our third option, we've specified a super-safe font in Arial. It's available on both Mac and PC, and on many other devices, too. As a last resort, we've requested a sans-serif font if none of our named fonts are available.

This list of font options ensures that the page will degrade gracefully, and will enable us to express our design preferences while working within the limitations of the site visitor's available fonts.

All Windows	Vista onwards	Windows 7
Arial	Calibri	*Gabriola*
Impact	Cambria	Segoe UI Light
Times New Roman	Consolas	**Segoe UI Semibold**
Courier New	Constantia	
Tahoma	Candara	**Windows 8**
Comic Sans	Meiryo	Calibri Light
Verdana	Corbel	
Georgia	Segoe UI	
Garamond		

Left: A selection of the fonts available in Windows. Each font name is formatted using that font.

Embedding fonts in web pages

You could send your chosen fonts over the Internet with the web page. Two things have hampered the progress of this approach:

- The first is that font creators don't necessarily want their fonts distributed over the Internet, and, for that reason, many fonts cannot be embedded without breaching copyright law.

- The second challenge is that browsers have implemented font embedding in different ways and at different times, making it a complex undertaking.

New services are becoming established that aim to solve both these problems. They enable you to buy a license for using a particular font on your website, and they then send it out to each of your visitors from their servers when it's needed. These services can also simplify the process of embedding the font, so that you don't have to cater for different browsers.

A subscription might be worthwhile if you plan to make extensive use of unusual typography. Font services include Fontdeck (**www. fontdeck.com**), Typekit (**www.typekit.com**), and the free Google Fonts service (**www.google.com/fonts**).

If it's important to use a particular font, then you could create an image that depicts the text and put that in your web page. You should limit this to something like a company logo and certainly shouldn't use it for more than a few words. It slows the website, is less accessible, and it can't be indexed by search engines.

Popular fonts on the Mac include Helvetica, Lucida Grande, Geneva, Monaco, Courier, Times, Arial, Verdana, Georgia, Baskerville, and Times New Roman.

There are three main units of measurement. Pixels are used for line widths, spaces and images. Ems are measurements of the size of the text. 1em is the height of the text in the current font. You can use em for the size of boxes, margins and padding, so that they change if the user increases the text size. You can also use percentages, for if you want a box to take up 30% of the available space, for example.

If you need to change three sides to one value, and the fourth to another, do this: Change all the sides to the most-used value. Then style the odd-one-out. When there is a conflict, the later rule overrides the earlier one. For example: margin: 1em; margin-left: 0.5em;

Padding, border and margin

Every HTML element (including paragraphs, headings, and sections marked up with <div> tags) has a padding, a border, and a margin. This is known as the box model.

If you had an HTML paragraph that contained the word "Hello", those properties would be arranged around the HTML element like this:

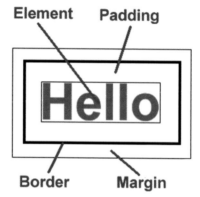

This is how the different elements can be used:

- The padding controls how much space there is between the element and its border. You can add padding equally around the element, or you can have uneven padding on the top, bottom, left and right edges.

- The margin controls how much space there is between the border and the next element. You can add a margin below a paragraph, for example, to create some empty space before the next paragraph begins. You might put a margin around a picture to offset it slightly from the text beside it.

- The border is a line on any or all sides of the element. That line can be any color and thickness and can use a number of different styles. You might add a thin line underneath a heading to create a horizontal rule under it, or you might put a box around a whole section so that it stands out. More often than not, an element will have no visible border added to it. The background color of an element fills the space up to its border, including its padding.

There are several different border properties you can change:

Property	What it means and example usage
border-width	You can use the values thin, medium or thick, but people usually specify an exact width in pixels. `border-width: 2px;`
border-color	`border-color:black;`
border-style	Describes the border's line: none, solid, dotted, dashed, double, groove, ridge, inset, outset. `border-style:solid;`
border	Used as a shorthand for all those properties, enabling you to combine them into one line. `border: 2px black solid;`

You can change these values for all four sides at once by using those properties, in the form shown in the table, or you can specify a particular side (top, bottom, left, right). For example: border-bottom-width, border-left-color, or border-right-style. The border doesn't have to look the same all the way around.

As an example, let's look at how you can use the border properties to put a red dotted line above and below your <h2> headings, as the screengrab below shows:

```
h2 { border-top: red 2px dotted;
border-bottom: red 2px dotted; }
```

This is a Heading 2

The descender on the letter g in that heading looks rather close to the border. What if we wanted to create some extra space between the text and the bottom border, and decided the heading should be indented slightly on the left? This extra CSS for the h2 style declaration would do the trick:

```
padding-left:0.5em; padding-bottom: 0.25em;
```

If you wanted to create some space between the heading and the body copy under it, you could set the margin-bottom to 1em.

Beware

There is probably some unknown amount of padding and margin around your element already, because browsers apply different default margins and padding. CSS frameworks usually include a reset style sheet to clear all these defaults (see page 132).

Below: Examples of border styles

Solid

Dotted

Dashed

Double

Groove

Ridge

Inset

Outset

117

Styling with class

Once you've marked up where the different chunks of content on your web page begin and end using <div> tags, you can style them by referencing their class names in the style sheet. You style class names in a similar way to how you style HTML tags, except that you use a full stop to tell the browser you're referencing a class:

Keep your class names short and meaningful. You're not allowed to use a space in a class name.

```
.classname { property: value; }
```

If you had a class name of "header" in your HTML, like this:

```
<div class="header">Header HTML goes here</div>
```

You would style it in your CSS like this:

```
.header { border: 2px black solid; color:black; }
```

Adding classes to other tags

You can use classes to apply different styles to the same HTML element on different parts of the page, too. For example, you might want product photos to have a thick border, but your thumbnail pictures to have a thin one. To do that, you could define two different classes of image. In your HTML, you would add a class definition to your image. If you had a class called thumbnail, for example, your image tag might look like this:

```
<img src="pottery.jpg" width="150" height="50"
alt="selection of handmade pottery" class="thumbnail">
```

A tag is used to mark up your HTML content and has pointed brackets. A selector is used in CSS to choose what you want to style. A class is used to identify different elements of the web page, for the purposes of styling them. For example, you could use a class to identify advertising boxes in the web page.

Complex selectors

To save having to add class names to every tag, you can also select a combination of classes and tags. If you decided you wanted the links in your body copy to be underlined, but those in your header not to be, it would be time consuming to add class names to so many links. You could, in that case, select all the <a> tags inside the <div> with the class name of header, like this:

```
.header a { text-decoration:none; }
```

Setting the text-decoration property to none turns off underlining, so this short snippet of CSS takes the underlining off all the <a> tags in the header <div> without needing to add classes to any of those links. This is a powerful web design tool, and gives you the flexibility to easily change how HTML tags are presented on different parts of the web page.

Advanced CSS selectors

Keep these advanced selectors in reserve, just in case you come across a challenging design problem they can solve.

Applying more than one class to an element

It is possible to apply more than one class in a tag. You just list all the classes you want to apply in the HTML tag and separate them with a space, like this:

```
<p class="biography sidebar">Biography goes here</p>
```

The browser will then apply the CSS style rules for the classes biography and sidebar.

Choosing a tag and class combination

If you want to, you can select a combination of a tag and a class, so that only tags with a particular class name will be styled. For example, you could select:

```
p.sidebar { color: #0000ff; }
```

This turns the text blue in a paragraph with the class name "sidebar", but it ignores any other tags that have that class, and also ignores any <p> tags that do not have that class.

Selecting by ID

As well as giving an HTML element a class, you can give it an ID. You've already met the ID attribute when creating forms. An ID must be applied only once on each web page, whereas classes can be reused many times on the page. You can choose to use a class just the once, though, so you might not need to use IDs at all. You add an ID to your HTML like this:

```
<div id="advertbox">Advertising goes here</div>
```

To style an ID, use #idname, like this:

```
#advertbox { color:black; }
```

Styling HTML5 selectors

Note that the new HTML tags for defining page structure in a document are ordinary tags and not class names. So, if you are using the HTML5 <nav> tag to define your navigation bar, you don't need to put a full stop before it in the CSS:

```
nav { style definitions go here }
```

For a full description of the selectors available, see the W3C CSS specification. There's a link to it on this book's section of my website, at www.sean.co.uk and at www.ineasysteps. com/resource-centre/ downloads under CSS, CSS3 and Web Design in easy steps.

119

You can select tags inside tags, too, using a similar syntax to the class and tag combination here. For example:

```
ul li { color:red; }
```

will select all the <li> tags in an unordered list, and exclude those in an ordered list.

Creating a simple layout

Now that you know how to apply different styles to different parts of the web page, we can look at how we can create a simple page layout using CSS. I'll show you how to make a layout that has a sidebar on the left that is 200 pixels wide, and a header and footer. We'll center our box of content on the screen, too.

1 Mark up your HTML as shown at the top of page 103, using <div> sections with class names of wrapper, header, sidebar, article, pullquote and footer.

2 In your CSS, change the background-color property for each section to something different. This is an optional step, and you'll almost certainly change it back later, but it helps you to see the margin and padding on each section of the page while you're working on your layout. I'm using blue for the wrapper, yellow for the header, red for the sidebar, white for the article, and green for the footer. My page, so far, looks a bit basic...

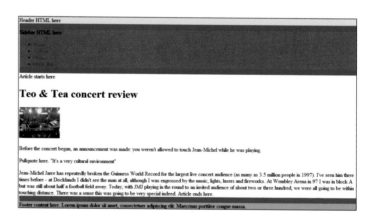

The blue lines you can see in this picture are where the wrapper is showing through. It's because the browser has automatically applied some margin where each <div> ends.

Percentages are calculated relative to the containing element. For example, a box with a width of 30% inside a <div> will be 30% of the width of the <div>. If your wrapper has a width of 90%, it will fill 90% of the screen width, because there is no containing element.

3 Long lines of text can be hard to read, so let's limit the width of our web page on the screen. You can set a width using pixels (e.g. 700px), percentages (eg 90%) or ems. If we set it using ems, then the page will get wider as the user enlarges the text, which helps to preserve the layout, even if the text gets much larger than we prefer.

```
.wrapper {background-color:blue; width:40em; }
```

4 Now we want to center our content on the screen. The way to do this is to set the left and right margins to be automatic. Older browsers don't support this well, though, so to get them to center our text, we have to use a bit of a hack. We center the text of the <body> tag, which has the effect of centering our content box in those browsers. Then we make the text left-aligned within our .wrapper <div>.

```
body { text-align: center; }
.wrapper {
background-color:blue;
width: 40em; text-align:left;
margin-left: auto; margin-right: auto;
}
```

5 Let's add some padding to our .wrapper. It will help us to see where the wrapper is, and will give us some space between the content and any border we want to put around all of it later. In our .wrapper CSS declarations, we need to add padding: 8px; and then our web page looks like this:

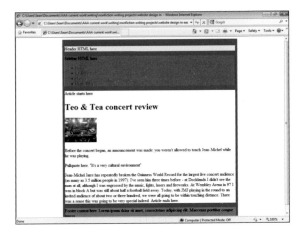

6 The edges of the boxes are tight against the text, so, to create some breathing space, add "padding: 8px;" to the style declarations for .header, .article, .sidebar and .footer.

You can find all kinds of hacks online that help you cater for the quirks of different browsers. Don't get caught up in trying to make everything look the same, though, otherwise you'll end up with really messy and complicated CSS. The important thing is that the design works and is usable, not that it's always identical.

121

The text-align property can also be used to align non-text elements, such as images.

...cont'd

7 The next step is to move the sidebar so that it appears to the left of the article, and not above it. To do that, we specify its width and then use a CSS property called float. This is what the CSS for our sidebar looks like now:

```
.sidebar{ background-color:red;
padding:8px;
width:200px; float:left; }
```

The resulting web page now looks like this:

Hot tip

By coloring your boxes, as we have here, you can see if any boxes are overlapping because you've set the wrong margins.

Beware

When your sidebar is longer than your article, your footer could appear underneath the article instead of at the bottom of the page. To avoid this, give the .footer a rule of clear:both;
If you intend to style the .wrapper container, you will need to use a hack to stop the sidebar spilling out of it. Check online for the "clearfix" solution.

8 As you can see, our text goes underneath the sidebar and we want our sidebar to take up a whole column, and have blank space underneath it if it finishes short of the main article. To achieve that, we add a margin to the left of the .article in its CSS. The margin needs to be 216 pixels, because the left hand column is 200 pixels wide plus 8 pixels of padding on each side of it.

```
.article
{
background-color:white;
padding:8px;
margin-left:216px;
}
```

Styling the content

Our two column layout is now finished and looks like this:

Once you have the layout working, you can start to style the web page. This template can be used to create a wide range of different visual effects. For example, you could make all the backgrounds white, so that the text appears to be neatly arranged in a continuous white space on the screen.

You could use borders at the bottom of the header, left of the article and top of the footer, to divide up the sections. You could also color the sections differently so they appear to be in colored boxes. You could make your web page "pop" out of the screen a little by setting the background to be a darker color.

You can also change the fonts and text colors for the different sections. Within the article, you could make the pullquote draw the eye by giving it a margin all around, a larger text-size of 1.3em and a font-style of italic. You could make all the photos appear on the right, using:

```
.article img { float:right; }
```

To offset your page from the top of the browser window, add a margin-top value to the wrapper class in your CSS.

123

You can incorporate your styles in an external CSS file, or put them between <style> and </style> tags in the header of your HTML file. If you use an external CSS file, you can share the same style sheet across multiple web pages.

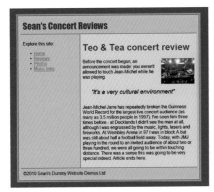

Left: two basic examples of how our simple layout could be styled.

Printer-friendly pages

Have you ever printed a web page, only to find that the end of each line is missing and you have three extra pages of adverts and navigational images that make no sense on paper? Don't let this happen on your website! CSS offers the perfect solution.

To create a style sheet to make your pages print cleanly, follow these steps:

1 Create a copy of your normal style sheet and save it as print.css. This will be your print style sheet.

2 Edit your print style sheet. Identify any sections of the page that shouldn't be printed. That might include adverts or entire sidebars or navigation sections. To stop these appearing, delete all the style declarations for them and replace them with display:none;. For example:

```
.advertbox { display:none; }
```

3 Check for any style declarations that won't work in print. Pay particular attention to any width declarations that might force the page to be wider than a piece of paper. Strip out excessive use of color that will waste ink.

4 Hopefully, you won't have to modify your HTML. If there's something you'd like to suppress from printing that is not already marked up as a section, you might need to add <div> and </div> tags around it so that you can stop it printing out. You can give these new sections the same class (eg "dontprint"). Set that class to display:none; in your print style sheet. Your screen style sheet does not need to be changed.

5 Modify your style sheet link in your HTML document(s), so that your main style sheet applies to your screen only. Link your print style sheet to your HTML document, too. Use this code:

```
<link href="main.css" rel="stylesheet"
type="text/css" media="screen">
<link href="print.css" rel="stylesheet"
type="text/css" media="print">
```

You can create style sheets for lots of different media, including screen (for desktop computer screens), braille (for tactile braille devices), speech (for speech synthesizers), handhelds (for pocket devices) and print (for printing out the web page).

If you don't declare a media for it when you link it from your HTML file, a style sheet is used for all media.

You can use @media rules in a style sheet to direct style declarations in it at a particular type of media. See the W3C site for more details.

List bullets and numbers

You can give your design some polish by changing the appearance of lists. The default bullets are fine and functional, but lack personality.

For ordered lists, which are usually numbered 1, 2, 3, you can choose, instead, to use roman numerals (upper or lower case) or to use letters (also upper or lower case). Generally, it's best to stick with numbers or simple letters, because they are most easily understood.

For bullets, there are three different styles. The default is the disc bullet, but you can also choose to use squares or (hollow) circles.

Hot tip

Bulleted lists help people to quickly understand your content.

Best of all, you can use your own image as a bullet, so you could have a bullet shaped like your logo, or of something linked to the theme of your site. In my example below, I've used musical notes as the bullet. Make sure you use something small and distinctive. The design needs to be simple, otherwise it can distract readers from the content it's supposed to point them towards.

To change the list style between any of the defaults, change the list-style-type CSS property. For example:

```
ul {list-style-type: square;}
ol {list-style-type: upper-alpha;}
```

To use an image for your list instead, you need to specify its path:

```
ul { list-style-image: url(images/notes.gif); }
```

list-style-type:disc	list-style-type:circle	list-style-type:square
• list item • list item two • list item three	○ list item ○ list item two ○ list item three	▪ list item ▪ list item two ▪ list item three
list-style-type:decimal	**list-style-type:lower-roman**	**list-style-type:upper-roman**
1. list item 2. list item two 3. list item three	i. list item ii. list item two iii. list item three	I. list item II. list item two III. list item three
list-style-type:lower-alpha	**list-style-type:upper-alpha**	**list-style-image: url(notes.gif);**
a. list item b. list item two c. list item three	A. list item B. list item two C. list item three	♪ list item ♪ list item two ♪ list item three

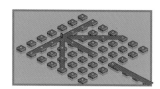

Above: Stu Nicholls created CSS Play (www.cssplay.co.uk) to showcase creative use of CSS. The maze above, for example, is built in pure CSS (without JavaScript). It uses a much more advanced application of the :hover pseudo-class used for the navbar here.

Hot tip

If you want to change the appearance of all the links in your document, just use:
a { css styles; }
To change the appearance of visited links, use:
a:visited {css styles; }

Creating a navbar with CSS

You can use CSS to turn a list of links into a set of navigation buttons. CSS enables you to offer visual feedback to the website visitor, so that they can see which link they are selecting, too.

1 If the style sheet isn't supported or available, your navigation would still make sense as a list of links. Add an unordered list of links to your HTML. Put your navigation links into a div with the class name of navbar. Your HTML should look like this:

```
<div class="navbar">
<ul>
<li><a href="home.htm">Home</a>
<li><a href="reviews.htm">Reviews</a>
<li><a href="photos.htm">Photos</a>
<li><a href="links.htm">Music links</a>
</ul>
</div>
```

2 There are two types of elements in HTML: block-level and inline. Block level elements are those that start on a new line, and they often contain inline elements. Block-level elements include <p>, <div>, <table> and headings. The unordered list is a block-level element, so we need to change our list items to display inline, so that our buttons appear beside each other. Add this line to your CSS:

```
.navbar ul li {display:inline;}
```

3 When viewed in your web browser, you should now see your links appear side by side without any bullets. To make these links look like buttons, style them with padding and a border:

```
.navbar a {
padding:8px;
color:white; background-color: #000000;
font-family:arial;
border-style:outset;
}
```

4 There are two problems with the navbar so far: the buttons are different widths depending on how much text they have on them, and the link text is still underlined. Set the width property so that it is the same for all the buttons. To remove underlining, set the text-decoration to none. Add these rules to your CSS for .navbar a:

```
text-decoration:none;
width:8em;
```

5 You can specify different or additional style rules that apply when the user is hovering over the link, or focused on it using the keyboard. To create a mouseover effect that shows the user when they are hovering over a link, or have selected it using the keyboard, add the following CSS. It changes the border from outset to inset (which looks like a button being pressed), and will also change the button's text from white to yellow:

```
.navbar a:hover,
.navbar a:active
{
border-style:inset;
color:yellow;
}
```

6 Finally, test your navbar. You should see that when you put the mouse over it, or when you use the tab key to select it with the keyboard, the button changes. My picture shows the finished navbar, with my mouse pointer hovering over the Reviews button.

It's a good idea to use the em unit for the width of the button, because if the user increases the text size, the button size will increase, too. Otherwise your text might not fit on the button when the user enlarges the text.

The parts of the selector :hover and :active are two examples of what are called pseudo-classes.

127

Do you need fancy positioning? You can put a margin around a <div> or an image, which often eliminates the need for relative positioning.

If you use position:fixed; the element you position will not move when the page scrolls. It stays on the screen as other content scrolls under it.

Advanced positioning

Most of the time, you can lay out pages using floats and margins. Occasionally, you might want to position something more precisely. There are two different ways you can position elements in HTML: relatively and absolutely.

- When you position something relatively, you tell the browser where you want it to go, compared to where the browser was going to put it anyway.

- When you position something absolutely, you tell the browser where it should go, usually measured from the top left of the browser window. You rarely need to know this, but if the thing you're positioning is inside something else that has been positioned, the object you are positioning is measured from that instead. This matters if you are positioning an image that is inside a <div> and the <div> has been absolutely positioned, for example.

With either approach, you typically give the browser an offset value from the top and from the left, like this:

```
.productimg
{ position: absolute; top: 20px; left: 20px; }

.productimg
{ position: relative; top: 15%; left: 35%; }
```

Specifying how things overlap

You can end up with elements positioned on top of each other if you use absolute or relative positioning. By default, those that are added later will appear on top. But you can change which elements appear to be on top of which other elements by setting a value for the z-index. This describes the third dimension (depth), and elements with higher values appear to be on top of those with lower values. You can set the z-index like this:

```
.productimg { z-index: 5; }
```

Other ways to specify positions

You can use negative values too, so if you want to position something 50 pixels to the left using relative positioning, declare a left offset of -50px. Similarly, a negative offset from the top in relative positioning can be used to place something above its usual position.

You can also position things from the bottom and the right. This could be used to position something in the bottom right corner of the screen:

```
position: absolute;
bottom: 2em;
right: 2em;
```

Percentage positioning

One thing to look out for: If you use a percentage for positioning, it is calculated relative to the containing block. If you're relatively positioning an image inside a <div> using percentages, for example, they will be calculated according to the width and height of the <div>, and not the image.

Left: Three overlapping images, placed using absolute positioning. They were added to the page in the order left to right.

Left: Those same images with z-index values of 10, 5 and 0 applied (from left to right).

You don't need to have a visible border. You can have the background color fill the area up to the rounded border, even when the border is not visible.

Look!
No border!

Hot tip

You can also use em or % values to specify the border-radius. More advanced features of border-radius enable elliptical corners.

CSS3 techniques

CSS3, the latest version of CSS, provides some effects you can use to enhance the appearance of your pages. Remember that older browsers might not support these techniques, so people might see a more basic design if they're using an old browser.

Rounded corners
The border-radius property enables you to round off the corners on an element. It can be particularly effective when applied to a box of content or an image. Here's an example usage:

```
border-radius: 8px;
```

CSS3 gives you
rounded corners
on your boxes.

You can specify a different radius for each corner if you wish:

```
border-top-left-radius: 8px;
border-top-right-radius: 2px;
border-bottom-right-radius: 12px;
border-bottom-left-radius: 4px;
```

As a shorthand, you can give four values for the border-radius. You start in the top-left corner, and then work your way around clockwise (top-left, top-right, bottom-right, bottom-left):

```
border-radius: 8px 2px 12px 4px;
```

If you specify just two values for the border-radius, the first is used for the top-left and bottom-right, and the second is used for the other two corners:

```
border-radius: 20px 40px;
```

Adding text shadows

You can add shadows to an element to give a sense of depth to it. This can be tiring to read for body text, but works well for headings and for other small chunks of text. The CSS to add a shadow to text looks like this:

```
text-shadow: 2px 2px 2px gray;
```

The four values are:

- **The horizontal offset for the shadow.** Use a positive number for a shadow to the right, and a negative one for a shadow on the left.

- **The vertical offset for the shadow.** Positive numbers are below the element and negative numbers are above it.

- **The amount of blur on the shadow.** Use 0 for a crisp shadow. Higher numbers give fuzzier shadows.

- **The final value is the shadow color.** I've used a color name here, but you can specify a color number instead.

You can use text-shadow to make 3D text for viewing with red/green 3D glasses. There is a tutorial at www.sean. co.uk/a/webdesign/3d/ css-text-shadow- anaglyph.shtm

Text shadow

Adding box shadows

There is also a property you can use to add a shadow to a whole element, such as a div. It is called box-shadow, and uses the same four values as text-shadow. It can make boxes of text appear to pop out of the page. For example:

```
box-shadow: 2px 2px 2px black;
```

which gives the result shown here (right).

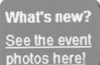

What's new?
See the event
photos here!

Degrading gracefully

On a browser that doesn't support rounded corners or box shadows, those features aren't shown, but the website functionality still works.

What's new?
See the event
photos here!

Next steps with CSS

The basic rules of CSS aren't that hard. It takes time to master how the different properties can be used together to create a complete website design, though, so this has just been a rapid tour through CSS to get you started.

This chapter doesn't cover all the capabilities of CSS. The W3C website (www.w3c.org) has a full list. Don't forget that those in the newer CSS3 specification are not well supported in some browser versions.

One of the challenges is that browsers differ in which CSS rules they understand, and how they interpret them. The good news is that you're unlikely to discover any new problems, so solutions can usually be found online. Basic layouts are unlikely to cause major display problems in any of the browsers in popular use.

One way you can speed up your website development and benefit from the experience of advanced CSS developers is to use a framework. Popular frameworks include Blueprint (download it at **www.blueprintcss.org/**), the Yahoo User Interface CSS (**http://developer.yahoo.com/yui/**), and the 960 Grid System (**http://960.gs/**). The 960 grid system also includes grids you can use for prototyping and planning.

Frameworks provide a set of pre-written style sheets that you can use in your website. They typically include a reset style sheet that cancels all the default CSS values that browsers apply, so that you don't come to rely on defaults that might not be present on other browsers. They also make it easier to do grid-based layouts, where all the elements on the page are aligned to an invisible underlying grid. Frameworks make it much easier to create professional layouts, but you'll still need to understand CSS to use them. It's worth spending some time creating your own style sheets, to familiarize yourself with CSS, first.

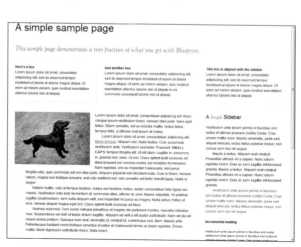

Left: The kind of sophisticated layouts Blueprint can help create.

You can check the quality of your CSS using the W3C validator at http://jigsaw.w3.org/css-validator/

Reference: text formatting

Property	Valid values
font-family	A list of named fonts. If font names have more than one word, enclose them in quotes. A generic type: serif / sans-serif / monospace / cursive / fantasy
font-size	A percentage: for example, 150% An em value: for example, 1.5em A size description: xx-small / x-small / small / medium / large / x-large / xx-large Browsers differ in their implementation of these size descriptions. For best results, set font-size using em or % measurements.
font-style	italic / normal
font-weight	bold / normal
font	This is a shorthand way of formatting fonts. For example: `p {font: bold italic Palatino, serif}`
text-align	left / right / center / justify
text-indent	An em value: for example, 3em A percentage: for example, 5% Sets an indent for the first line of text.
text-transform	capitalize / uppercase / lowercase / none You can use this setting to change the case of text. Capitalize puts the first character of each word into uppercase. The uppercase and lowercase values change all characters.
text-decoration	underline / overline / line-through / none
color	A color number or name, eg #FF0000 or red
list-style-type	disc / circle / square / decimal / lower-roman / upper-roman / lower-alpha / upper-alpha
list-style-image	Path to your image. For example: `ul { list-style-image: url(dot.gif); }`

Hot tip

The font-size is relative to its current size, and not necessarily relative to the default size. If a <div> has a font-size of 150%, and a paragraph in it has a font-size of 200% applied to it, the text in the paragraph will be twice as large as the rest of the <div> content, which will be one and a half times as large as text content outside the <div>. The same would apply if the sizes were declared as 1.5em and 2em.

Beware

Font size is often measured in points (pt) in applications like word processing. Note that, while it is possible to set an absolute size for text (e.g. 12pt) on your website, this will stop the user from being able to adjust the text size to their preferences, so this should be avoided.

Reference: backgrounds

Property	Valid values
background-color	A color number or name, eg #FF0000 or red
background-image	url(path to image file) Example: `body{background-image:url(images/train.jpg);}`

background-position	One or more word values:
	top / bottom / right / left / center
	
	Two measurements for how far from the left and top of the element the background should start. For example, 8px 16px
	
	Two percentages for the x and y position, e.g. 10% 20%. This would place the point that is 10% across and 20% down the image, at the point that is 10% across and 20% down the element that the background is in. A value of 0% 0% aligns the background with the top left corner of the element. 100% 100% aligns it with the bottom right corner.
	
	Example:
	`body {background-position: 8px 16px; }`
	`body {background-position: top center; }`
	`body {background-position: 30% 50%; }`

background-attachment	fixed / scroll This property dictates whether the background scrolls with the element's content or stays fixed.
background-repeat	repeat / repeat-x / repeat-y / no-repeat This property dictates whether the background image is repeated. repeat-x and repeat-y enable you to limit the repetition to the horizontal or vertical direction.
background	A shorthand property for the other background properties. For example: `.trainpara {background: url("train.jpg") black repeat fixed;}`

Hot tip

If you don't want text to appear on top of a background image that fills part of your content box, set padding on the box to offset where the text starts.

Beware

If you use a background-image, make sure you also set a background-color that contrasts with the foreground color. Otherwise, your text might be unreadable when the image is unavailable or unsupported on the user's device.

Reference: layout

Positioning

Property	Valid values
float	left / right
clear	left / right / both Specifies which side of an element floating is not allowed.

position	absolute / relative
	Plus is a measurement for the offset to the right and down. Negative numbers are valid. Absolute positions are relative to the top left corner of the screen unless inside another positioned element. Relative positions compared to where the element would normally have been on the page.
	
	Examples:
	`position: absolute; top:20px; left 20px;`
	`position: relative; top:15%; left:35%;`

z-index	A number When elements overlap, the z-index determines which is in front. Higher numbers are in front of lower numbers. You can set negative values.
overflow	visible / hidden / scroll Determines what happens to excess content, for example, if the size of a box is set using a fixed width and height and the text doesn't fit. This can often be avoided by sizing elements containing text using em measurements.

Sizing

Property	Valid values
width	A measurement or percentage, e.g. 8px, 30em or 70%. The percentage width is specified relative to the containing element. For example, a <div> with a class of .wrapper that has a width of 70% and is the first object in the <body>, will have the width of 70% of the body.
height	A measurement or percentage, e.g. 8px, 30em or 70%. See notes for width, above.

You don't have to use all of these properties. The width and height, for example, are automatically calculated, unless you specify them.

Use the clear property to force an element underneath a sidebar that has been floated.

There are also CSS properties for min-width, max-width, min-height and max-height which set the minimum and maximum desired dimensions. These weren't supported in IE until IE7.

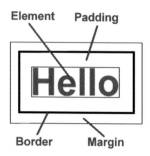

Above: The box model shows how padding, margins, and borders apply to an element.

Hot tip

Set the left and right margins to auto to center the element.

...cont'd

Spacing

Property	Valid values
margin	auto A measurement or percentage, e.g. 8px or 30%. The percentage margin applied to an element is calculated according to the size of its container, and not the size of the element itself. For example, if a <div> with a class of .article is inside a <div> with a class of .wrapper and has a right margin of 20%, its right margin will be 20% of the width of .wrapper. Different values can be set for margin-top, margin-bottom, margin-left and margin-right.
padding	A measurement or percentage, calculated based on the containing element (see notes for margin, above). Different values can be set for padding-top, padding-bottom, padding-left and padding-right.
line-height	A number to be multiplied by the font size (e.g. 1.5), a percentage of the font size (e.g. 150%), or a measurement (eg 1.5em).
letter-spacing	A measurement of spacing between letters. Negative values can be used to close the default gap. e.g. 1.5em or -1.5em.
word-spacing	As for letter-spacing, above, but it applies to spaces between words.

Borders

Property	Valid values
border-width	thin / medium / thick Width in pixels, such as: border-width: 2px;
border-color	A color number or name, eg #FF0000 or red
border-style	none / solid / dotted / dashed / double / groove / ridge / inset / outset
border	Used as a shorthand for all those properties, enabling you to combine them into one line. `.wrapper { border: 2px black solid; }`

Reference: pseudo-classes

Property	How it is used
:active	Used for behavior of links when the user has tabbed to them using the keyboard, or is clicking on them using the mouse.
:hover	Used for behavior when the user is hovering over an element. To make links appear highlighted in yellow when the mouse is over them, use: `a:hover { background-color: yellow; }`
:link	Used to style unvisited links, e.g.: `a:link { color:blue; }`
:visited	Used to style visited links, e.g.: `a:visited { color:purple; }`

:focus	Styles elements when they are accepting text input. For example, to make form fields go yellow when they are in use (see picture, right):
	`input:focus, select:focus,`
	`textarea:focus`
	`{ background-color: yellow; }`

:first-letter	Used to style the first letter in an element. For example, to enlarge the first letter of each paragraph in any <div> with a class name of article, use: `.article p:first-letter {font-size:2em;}`
:first-line	Used to style the first line in an element. Usage is the same as for first-letter.

:after
:before
	Used to add some text content before or after a particular element. For example, to add the word "Warning" before any paragraph with the class of warning, use:
	`p.warning:before { content: "Warning" ;}`
	
	You can also add an image using its path:
	`p.warning:before {`
	`content: url(warningbox.jpg); }`
	
	Remember that this only works where style sheets are available, and where the browser supports these pseudo-elements. Don't depend on this to add important information to the web page.

137

To help you remember what your CSS does, you can add comments in it, like this:

/*This is a comment*/

Comments are ignored by the browser. To disable a chunk of CSS temporarily, while you experiment, turn it into a comment:

/* float:right;
margin-left: 8px; */

Beware

Remember that not all browsers support these properties. Take particular care with the opacity and background images. Where these are not supported by the browser, your visitor might not see something you intend them to see.

Hot tip

The website www.caniuse.com tells you which browsers support which features of CSS3 and HTML5.

Reference: CSS3

Property	How it is used
border-radius	Specifies how rounded the corners on an element should be. If you provide four values, they are used for the top-left, top-right, bottom-right, and bottom-left in that order. If two values are provided, the first one is for the top-left and bottom-right, and the second is for the other two corners. If one value is provided, it applies to all four corners. `border-radius: 8px 2px 12px 4px;`
text-shadow	Adds a drop shadow to text. The four values provided are the horizontal offset (negative number is left, positive is right); the vertical offset (negative number is up, positive is down); the amount of blur; and the shadow color. e.g.: `text-shadow: 2px 2px 2px gray;`
box-shadow	This property adds a shadow to an element, such as a box of text or an image. It uses the same values as text-shadow above. `box-shadow: 2px 2px 2px black;`
opacity	The opacity property determines how transparent an element is. The value goes from 1 (which is opaque, or normal) to 0 (which is so transparent it's invisible). `opacity: 0.75;`

background-image	In CSS3, you can specify multiple background images, and separate them with commas.
	
	Here is an example of how you might use that and indicate how the image should be repeated and where it should start:
	
	`background: url(logo.gif) no-repeat top left,`
	`url(horiz.gif) repeat-x bottom left,`
	`url(vert.gif) repeat-y top right;`

8 JavaScript for interactive pages

JavaScript enables you to make your web pages interactive. You can check that forms have been completed correctly, update the screen with text or photos; display randomly chosen special offers; and add sophisticated animation and formatting effects to your pages. In this chapter, you'll learn the basics and discover some handy code you can adapt for your website.

What is JavaScript?

While HTML is used to describe the structure of your content, and CSS lets you describe its appearance, JavaScript gives you the power to make the computer perform actions. It is a simple programming language that you can use to make your web page interactive.

You can, for example:

For security reasons, JavaScript is limited to working within the browser. That means that it can't interfere with the website visitor's computer, and access the hard disk, for example.

- Update the screen contents after the page has downloaded. You might add new information that has become available since the web page first downloaded, or might show additional information that the user requests. Webmail service Gmail uses JavaScript to show you new messages that come in, without you having to refresh the web page, for example.

- Make it easier for visitors to use forms by checking for any errors before the form information is sent to the server. You can provide immediate feedback so that users don't waste time waiting for the server to respond.

- Hide or reveal web page content. You might, for example, have different tabbed sections of content, which the user can display on the current web page by clicking on a tab.

- Set cookies on the computer, which are small text files that are stored on a user's computer so that they can be identified when they visit again.

- Respond to user action, including clicks on the page. Some people even use JavaScript to create arcade games.

To tell website visitors who don't have JavaScript what they're missing, put a message between <noscript> and </noscript> tags in your HTML. Anything between these tags will only be presented to the user when JavaScript isn't available.

JavaScript is widely supported, but users of assistive devices might not be able to use it. Search engines can also struggle with it. For that reason, you should avoid using it for navigation and should ensure that your website still functions well with JavaScript disabled. Take particular care that appropriate alternative content is provided if JavaScript is used to convey information or content.

You also need to take care with updates to parts of the screen that the user might not be looking at. People using screen magnifiers can only see a small part of the screen at a time, but even people using normal browsers can have problems if you update the top of the page with something important after they've already scrolled it out of view.

...cont'd

JavaScript is considerably more complex than HTML and CSS, so I can only introduce you to the basics here and give you some example code you can cut, paste and edit to your requirements. This chapter gives you enough knowledge to experiment with scripts you find online, and to start making your own simple effects for your webpages.

I'll show you how to respond to user actions, such as mouse movements; how to hide and reveal different parts of the web page; how to change the content or design of the web page; how to tailor your website content to the month, day of the week or time of day; how to validate that form data has been entered correctly; how to open a new window; how to add a box of randomly selected content to your web page; and how to create a photo slideshow. I'll conclude with some quick demonstrations of jQuery, a JavaScript library that can make it easier for you to achieve impressive effects.

It might sound like a lot, but we're only scratching the surface of what's possible with JavaScript.

Do you need to learn JavaScript? Not necessarily. JavaScript is an important foundation for websites that require updating in real time, or that need to wow their visitors with interactive effects. But many websites can work without it. If you do learn how to create JavaScript, though, you'll soon spot opportunities to use it to make your website more interactive, useful and fun. Once you've mastered HTML and CSS, JavaScript is the next logical step in building your website and your web design skills.

Above: Snapple, Skyhigh and Flatland are three JavaScript games created by Brent Silby. You can play these games, and several others, in your browser at www.def-logic.com

141

Made by The Man in Blue

Left: Cameron Adams (www.themaninblue. com) created his arcade game Bunny Hunt using JavaScript. Play it at http://www. themaninblue.com/ experiment/BunnyHunt/

How to add JavaScript

Like HTML and CSS, you can write JavaScript using any text editor. There are two ways to add JavaScript to your web page.

 Put your JavaScript between HTML <script> tags. The JavaScript goes between the <head> and </head> tags of your HTML document, like this:

```
<head>
<script type="text/javascript">
alert('Hello!');
</script>
</head>
```

If you add that example to your web page, you'll see that, when it opens, an alert box displays "Hello!". You have to click OK to make it go away. The line alert('Hello!'); is the JavaScript that makes that box appear. The rest of the code is the HTML used to add JavaScript to your page.

2 Add an external JavaScript file. You can put your JavaScript commands into a separate text file and give it a .js extension, and then use a <script> tag to add it into a web page. That means you can share the same JavaScript code across different web pages, or even across different websites. Your website will load more quickly if you add your external JavaScript file at the bottom of your HTML file, just before the closing </body> tag. Here's the code to add an external JavaScript file called alertbox.js:

```
<script src="alertbox.js"
type="text/javascript"></script>
```

Your alertbox.js file could be just one line:

```
alert('Hello!');
```

You can add an external JavaScript file that's on somebody else's server like this:

```
<script src="http://www.example.com/alertbox.js"
type="text/javascript"></script>
```

Services like Google Analytics will provide some code for you to paste into your web page that looks very much like this.

Creating functions

Web designers often create functions, which are groups of JavaScript commands that should be executed (or carried out) in sequence. All these commands can then be executed by just telling the browser the name of the function to use, and when to use it. There are several benefits to using functions:

- It makes it easier to reuse JavaScript on a web page. You can run the same function under different circumstances, and could even do slightly different things with the function each time. You could use the same reveal function to reveal two different boxes, for example.

- Functions enable you to control when the commands are executed. If your JavaScript is outside a function, the browser will try to run it as soon as possible. Most of the time, you'll want to use JavaScript to respond to something that's happening on the web page, so being able to defer JavaScript actions until the right time is extremely valuable.

- Functions make it easier to understand what your JavaScript code does, so you can maintain and adapt it more easily.

Here's an example of a function that displays two alert messages. I've given the function the name "welcome". Because of the way the alert command works, the visitor has to click the OK button to get each alert box to go away. Alert boxes are good for testing and learning, but they're irritating for users, so I don't recommend using them on real web pages.

```
function welcome()
{
alert('Hello!');
alert('Thanks for visiting my site!');
}
```

A function has two ordinary brackets at the end of its name, and curly braces are used to mark the start and end of that function. You can put this JavaScript code (from the word "function" down to the closing curly bracket) in the header of your HTML page, or in an external file, where you previously put the single alert command.

You can see how the alert command works more clearly now: the bit between the single quotes is what appears in the alert box on screen. You can change this to anything you want.

Beware

Each JavaScript command should end with a semi-colon. If your JavaScript doesn't work, check for any missing semi-colons.

Beware

If you want to include an apostrophe in the text of the alert box, you have to add a \ before it, because single quotes (which are the same character) are used to mark the start and end of the alert box content. Using a \ tells the browser that you really do want it to display an apostrophe:

alert('Sean\'s alert box');

Beware

The "Click this paragraph" is just an example. If you have to tell people where to click on a real web page, your interface is poorly designed.

Hot tip

In this example, the clickable area takes up all the space that the paragraph does, including the blank space at the end of the line. To see the area a paragraph takes up, change its background color. Avoid using mouseover events in a way that will make apparently blank screen areas behave unpredictably.

Responding to user actions

Now we have created our JavaScript function called welcome(), we need a way to trigger it. JavaScript is event-driven. That means JavaScript commands are usually triggered when something happens, such as somebody clicking a link or moving the mouse over a link or image.

Here are some simple steps you can follow to add a JavaScript event to your web page:

1 Create your HTML in the usual way.

2 Find the part of the web page where you want to respond to a user action. If you want to respond to the mouse pointer touching a picture, find its <img> tag, for example. If you want to respond to a click on a paragraph, find its opening <p> tag. My HTML looks like this:

```
<p>Click this paragraph!</p>
```

3 Find the event name for the action you want to respond to. The table on the facing page shows a list of event names and what will trigger them. For example, let's respond to a mouse click on a particular paragraph, which means we'll be using onClick with our <p> tag.

4 Add the event name inside the brackets of the opening tag. It needs to go after the tag name and a space.

5 Add an equals sign, and put the JavaScript you want to execute in double quotes. That could be a function name, or could be a number of JavaScript commands, as long as there's a semi-colon after each one. Here's my finished tag:

```
<p onClick="welcome();">Click this paragraph!</p>
```

Now, when somebody clicks that paragraph, the welcome() function will be executed, which, if you created the function as described in this chapter, displays two alert boxes on screen.

...cont'd

Event name	What triggers it
onMouseOver	The mouse pointer rolls over something
onMouseOut	The mouse pointer rolls away again
onClick	Something is clicked
onFocus	The user enters a form field or uses the keyboard to select a link
onBlur	The user moves away from a form field or a link selected by keyboard
onChange	The user changes a form field, such as choosing a radio button, and then moves their focus away from that field
onLoad	The web page loads
onUnload	The user goes to a different page

You can use a timer to trigger an action. Use the setTimeout() command and give it the JavaScript to execute later, with the length of delay in milliseconds. For example:
setTimeout('welcome();', 1250);

Which tags can you use?

You can add the mouse events to most HTML tags, including <p>, <h1>...<h6>, <div>, <span>, <img>, <label>, <li>, <a> and <input>. You can add them to pretty much any tag you're likely to want to, in fact.

You can use onFocus and onBlur with tags for entering information and selecting options in forms; and <a> tags. onChange is only used with tags for entering information and selecting options in forms.

onLoad and onUnload should only be added to the <body> tag.

Adding actions to links

You could use onMouseOver and onMouseOut together to show and hide a pulldown menu on a navbar. Assuming you had functions called openmenu() and closemenu(), which show and hide the menu, your link tag might look like this:

```
<a href="books.htm" onMouseOver="openmenu();"
onMouseOut="closemenu();">Books</a>
```

When the mouse goes over the link, the openmenu() code will run. When the mouse goes away again, closemenu() will run. If the link is clicked, the browser opens the books.htm page as usual, so this link can still work if JavaScript isn't available.

Using an <a> tag with an onClick event makes it easy for people to see where they should click, because the clickable area will look like other links on the page. You need to disable the link destination, though. To do that, use href="javascript:;" It needs both a colon and a semi-colon before the closing double quotes.

Showing and hiding content

One of the most useful things you can do with JavaScript is to show or hide content on the page. You could, for example, filter information, so that users see a short summary or headline and then click to see more information on the same page. Alternatively, you could make forms easier to use by hiding irrelevant fields. If somebody selects a country outside the US, for example, you could hide the zip code box to avoid confusion. By using a timer, you could enable the page to update itself dynamically. You could make one "featured article" box disappear and be replaced by another instantaneously.

To show or hide content on your web page, follow these steps:

1 To tell the browser which content you would like to hide or reveal, wrap it in <div> and </div> tags and give it an ID in the opening tag, like this:

```
<div id="box1">Optional box</div>
```

2 Add a control to show the content when you want to. For example, you might use the heading above the box:

```
<h2 onClick="show('box1');">How can I apply?
</h2>
```

3 Add these two JavaScript functions to your web page:

```
function show(whichdiv)
{ document.getElementById(whichdiv).style.
display='block'; }
function hide(whichdiv)
{ document.getElementById(whichdiv).style.
display='none'; }
```

4 Change your <body> tag so that the section is hidden when the page loads using JavaScript. This ensures that those who do not have JavaScript can still see the content, but that the content is hidden from those with JavaScript when the page loads.

```
<body onLoad="hide('box1');">
```

5 Test it works as expected in your browser. Make sure it's obvious to users that they can click to reveal new content, otherwise they might not realize they're missing anything.

Hot tip

JavaScript isn't fussy about whether you use single quotes or double quotes. It won't work if you start something, like the content of an alert box, with one type and finish with another, though.

Hot tip

Using this code, you can have lots of boxes of optional content on the same page, as long as they have different IDs.

Hot tip

Each box of optional content can include as much HTML content as you wish, including pictures, links and other formatted content.

How it works

This is how the code works:

1 When somebody clicks on the heading, the browser uses the onClick action associated with the heading. That tells it to execute the show() function, and also passes it the name of the box we want to show, which is box1.

2 The way the show() function is defined in its first line means that it takes this box name and puts it in memory, in a place called 'whichdiv'. This is known as a variable, and is a handy way to store and keep track of information, such as which box we want to change.

3 The function uses getElementById to find the element in the document that has the same name as whatever is in the 'whichdiv' variable. In our example, that means it looks for the element called box1. Note that, because we're using a variable and not using the actual name of the element, we don't put single quotes around whichdiv.

4 The show() function then makes the CSS display property of that element be 'block', which is a visible style. The hide function will have changed it to 'none', which is what makes the content invisible.

Why do the show() and hide() functions use a variable? It means they are more flexible. You can use the same code to show or hide any number of different content sections by just passing a different ID to the function: such as show('box4'); hide('box3');

You can use this code as a template to make changes to other CSS properties of an element. You just change the property from "display" to whatever you want. To make the text go red, use:

```
document.getElementById(whichdiv).style.
color='#ff0000';
```

You could make a thick black border appear around an element by using this line of JavaScript:

```
document.getElementById(whichdiv).style.border='8px
black solid';
```

Jokebox

Why are there no aspirin in the jungle?

...Because the parrots eat 'em all. You can use this technique for fun features, like this random Jokebox I made for my website.

Beware

Get the capital letters in the right place in getElementById, otherwise it might not work.

Don't forget

If you are changing the style of the same thing people are mousing over or focusing on, it's easiest to do that using the :hover and :focus pseudo styles in CSS.

Adding a toggle routine

You can ask JavaScript to make some simple decisions about what it should do. This is commonly used for things like form validation, where the website only displays an error message if the form has been completed incorrectly. This is how conditional statements are structured:

```
if (test to be done)
{instructions to carry out if that condition is
satisfied}
else {instructions to carry out if condition isn't
satisfied}
```

We can use this simple decision making power to create a toggle function. This will show something that's hidden and hide something that's shown. The code looks like this:

```
function toggle(whichdiv)
{
if (document.getElementById(whichdiv).style.
display=='block')
{document.getElementById(whichdiv).style.
display='none';}
else
{document.getElementById(whichdiv).style.
display='block';}
}
```

It checks whether the display property is block (that is, visible), and, if so, it changes it to none (invisible). Otherwise, the display property must be none, already changing to block.

JavaScript uses two equals signs together when it's checking whether something is true (such as whether the display property is 'block', in this case). It uses one equals sign when it's changing something to be equal to something else.

Don't mix up your brackets! The if command uses round brackets around the things it's basing a decision on (such as whether the display property is 'block'), and then uses curly braces around the commands it will execute if those conditions are satisfied. Every opening bracket needs a closing bracket of the same type.

Right: the code for a frequently asked questions page, where you can click the questions to reveal the (heavily abbreviated!) answers. It also includes an example box of content that is toggled.

```
js show and hide togglebox scngrab.htm - Notepad
File  Edit  Format  View  Help
<html>
<head>
<script type="text/javascript">

function show(whichdiv)
{ document.getElementById(whichdiv).style.
display='block'; }

function hide(whichdiv)
{ document.getElementById(whichdiv).style.
display='none'; }

function toggle(whichdiv)
{
if (document.getElementById(whichdiv).style.display=='block')
{document.getElementById(whichdiv).style.display='none';}
else
{document.getElementById(whichdiv).style.display='block';}
}

</script>
</head>

<body onLoad="hide('answer1');hide('answer2');">

<h1>Frequently asked questions</h1>

<h2 onClick="show('answer1');">How can I apply?</h2>
<div id="answer1">To apply for this offer...</div>

<h2 onClick="show('answer2');">How much could I save?</h2>
<div id="answer2">Your potential savings will depend on...</div>

<h2 onClick="toggle('togglebox');">Click me to toggle the box
below</h2>
<div id="togglebox">This box is shown/hidden by clicking the heading
above it</div>

</body>
</html>
```

Simple form validation

One of the most popular uses of JavaScript is to check whether form data has been entered correctly. There are several things you can test:

- The length of information entered. For example, if the length is zero, then the field has been left blank.

- Whether something has been typed in that exactly matches what you're looking for.

- Whether a particular symbol or word has been entered as part of the information entered. For example, does an email address include an @ sign and a full stop?

- Whether a particular radio button or checkbox has been selected?

Friendly form validation

There are two ways you can validate your form. You can provide feedback as people are completing the form. You could, for example, check an email address as soon as it's been typed in and then show an immediate warning message if it's invalid. The advantage of this is that you can offer feedback where and when it's needed most. Alternatively, you can offer feedback when the whole form has been completed and the submit button has been pressed, perhaps highlighting any problem fields in red. The advantage of this is that users can have one pass through entering information and a second pass through fixing any problems, which might make the process seem quicker.

Two important guidelines will ensure that your validation is seen as helpful, not hectoring:

1. Publish the rules up-front. If a password has to be between eight and 15 characters, tell people before you ask them to make one up. You'll only annoy them if you tell them for the first time after they've typed it in.

2. Don't over-validate. Telling people their name or phone number is too long, or that their address is wrong, is annoying when they're right. Take particular care to ensure that long names and foreign addresses and phone numbers can be entered into your forms without triggering warnings.

You can find more advanced form validation scripts online, which will (for example) test that the @ sign and full stop are in the right places in the email address. Search the web for "form validation JavaScript".

149

Above: On my website, visitors can use a simple form to chat to a virtual version of me. It uses JavaScript to check for certain keywords in the text entered, so it can often appear to give an intelligent response. You can find it and my other JavaScript games at http://www.sean.co.uk/a/javascriptgames/index.shtm

Beware

I'm using alert() here as a handy shorthand, because it's easy to understand in the code. You should use a less intrusive way to warn the user, such as innerHTML, explained later in this chapter.

Don't forget

You can use maxlength in your HTML input tags to limit the number of characters someone can type into a text box, so you don't need to test for people entering too many characters.

Beware

Test your forms give the right messages by trying different inputs that match and don't match what you're testing for.

Checking text boxes

One of the simplest checks you can perform is to see whether a field has been left empty. You can do that by checking the length of the information in it.

You can add a JavaScript command to the form field using onBlur:

```
<input type="text" id="name" onBlur="validatename();">
```

You could use onChange to start the JavaScript, but the field starts off empty, so, if it's not changed, it will remain empty but the validation routine won't run. onBlur will trigger the JavaScript when somebody clicks on the form field or uses the keyboard to navigate to it, and then navigates away again. The result is that they'll be warned if their cursor enters that box, but they don't type anything into it before moving on.

Here's an example of what the validatename() function might look like:

```
function validatename()
{
if (document.getElementById('name').value.length<1)
{alert('Name is blank');}
}
```

If you want to check for a different minimum length, just change the 1 in that function. If you want to ensure that passwords are at least six characters, for example, change the 1 to a 6.

To check whether somebody has entered a particular word or name into a box, use this snippet of JavaScript in your validation function. It uses an alertbox to show a special greeting to people named Karen:

```
if (document.getElementById('name').value.
toLowerCase()=='karen')
{alert('Hello Karen!');}
```

The toLowerCase() part converts whatever is entered into the box to lower case before it is tested. That means the message will be shown whether somebody types in "Karen", "KAREN" or "karen". When you customize the code to your own needs, make sure you test for a match with the lower case version of the word or name (between the rounded brackets of the if statement), otherwise it will never trigger a message.

More advanced form tests

Converting the text to lower case before comparing it provides some flexibility, but what if somebody puts a space before or after their name? JavaScript won't consider that to be a perfect match for the name we're looking for, so it won't trigger the message.

Sometimes we want to check for a partial match, too, such as checking whether an @ sign occurs anywhere in the text entered. Assuming we have a text box with the ID of email, to check for the occurrence of one character inside an address, we use indexOf.

```
if (document.getElementById('email').value.
toLowerCase().indexOf('@')==-1) { alert('Email
addresses must have an @'); }
```

That can look a bit confusing, but this is how it works:

- **document.getElementById('email'):** This finds the element in the document with the ID of email, which is our text box.

- **.value:** This gets the content from that text box.

- **.toLowerCase():** This converts that content to lower case.

- **.indexOf('@'):** This checks whether the @ sign is in that content. It gives the number -1 if it isn't, otherwise, it gives a number that shows where it is in the email address. The numbers start at zero, so if the @ sign is the fifth character, it will output the number four.

- **if:** The if condition wrapped around it all tests whether the number output is -1, and, if it is, it shows the message warning people that the email address needs to have an @.

Has a checkbox been ticked?

You can test whether a checkbox has been ticked, too, so you could hide or reveal different parts of the form accordingly. Assuming you have a checkbox with an ID of options, this is how you test:

```
if (document.getElementById('options').checked==true)
{ code to show/hide options goes here }
```

You can use the same code to test whether a radio button with an ID of options has been selected. It feels more intuitive for content to appear or disappear when a box is ticked than when a radio button is selected, though.

The toLowerCase() part isn't necessary for this example, but it makes it easier for you to adapt the code to check a form field for particular letters or words.

You can use a select menu to restrict what people can enter when the options are limited (such as country names). If you do, you can check for an exact match without worrying about any spaces or odd capitalization.

Each form element needs to have a unique ID. Otherwise, your JavaScript might end up testing the wrong parts of the form.

Customizing by date

JavaScript enables you to see what the date and time is on the user's computer, so you can display special messages depending on the time of day, day of the week, or the month. Here's some code that will work out the date, month, day of the week and hour:

```
function the_date()
{today=new Date();temp=today.getDate();return temp;}

function the_month()
{today=new Date();temp=today.getMonth();return temp;}

function the_day()
{today=new Date();temp=today.getDay();return temp;}

function the_hour()
{today=new Date();temp=today.getHours();return temp;}
```

When you use these functions, they will give you a number, as the following table shows:

Function	Number returned
the_date()	Returns today's date (1-31)
the_month()	Returns the month number, where 0 is January and 11 is December
the_day()	Returns the day of the week, where 0 is Sunday, 1 is Monday, 2 is Tuesday, up to 6 for Saturday
the_hour()	Returns the hour from the time now (24 hour clock)

Displaying seasonal messages

You can use these simple functions to personalize your website experience a bit more. For example, if you want to show a different greeting depending on the time of day, you could use:

```
if (the_hour()<12) {alert('Good morning!');} else
if (the_hour()<18) {alert('Good afternoon!');} else
alert('Good evening!');
```

This works because of the order the tests are in. It checks whether the hour is less than 12, and only then does it check whether it's less than 18. To get to that point, we know it's more than 12, so we can confidently show a "Good afternoon!" message. If the hour is later than 18, it shows the "Good evening!" message. If you jumble those tests up, it won't work.

Hot tip

You can combine what you have learned about form validation with the number comparisons here to test numbers entered into forms. Add an input box in your web page HTML:

```
<input type="text" id="age">
```

You can then use JavaScript to display a message to under 18s:

```
if (document.getElementById('age').value<18)
{alert('Message for under 18s');}
```

Don't forget

You need to put your JavaScript functions between <script> tags in the header or in an external JavaScript file. If you get confused, download the sample code from my website.

What if you want to test for something that can't be arranged so elegantly, such as working out whether it's the weekend or not? You can add multiple tests inside the rounded brackets of the if statement. If you want an action to be taken when either of the conditions is true, you use || to combine them, like this:

```
if (the_day()==6 || the_day()==0) { alert('It\'s the
weekend!'); }
```

The table below shows all the comparisons you can make.

==	Equal to
!=	Not equal to
>	Greater than
<	Less than
>=	Greater than or equal to
<=	Less than or equal to

Updating the HTML content on screen

We've been using alert() as a handy shorthand in our examples, but you should update the content in the web page, rather than display a pop-up box, in nearly every case.

The problem with using hidden <div> sections for conditional content or error messages is that their content will still be presented to people who can't use JavaScript on their devices. If it's in the HTML, it'll be presented to the user when JavaScript isn't available. That's not what we want when it comes to error messages or conditional content. Instead, we can change the HTML content that is inside a <div> section. Imagine you have an empty <div> with the ID "msgs". You can change its content to something else, like this:

```
document.getElementById('msgs').innerHTML='Error
message';
```

Your error message can include any HTML tags you want. If you want to add to a section instead of replacing what is there, change the = sign to be += in the above example. You could then use the same box to report all your validation errors. You could combine the innerHTML method with the show() and hide() functions, so that your error message box isn't shown on screen until it has something in it, for example.

Hot tip

If you only want an action to be taken when both the conditions are true, you use && to combine them, in place of ||. You can combine more than two conditions at once, too.

Hot tip

If you don't mind about the size of the window, or the controls it has, you can use the target attribute in HTML to open a new window:
<a href="terms.htm" target="_blank">Terms (in new window)</a>

Beware

Warn people before opening a new window. It can be disorientating, especially to people using screenreaders.

Beware

Beware of popup blockers, which try to stop websites forcing unwanted advertising windows on visitors. They can also block windows that are part of the content.

Opening new windows

Sometimes it can be helpful to open a new window. If somebody is about to complete a form, for example, you don't want to take them to a new page to view the terms and conditions. It's better to open them in a new browser window, so they can read them, close the window then carry on with submitting the form. You open a window like this, giving it your own choice of name:

```
window.open('page or URL', 'windowname', 'options');
```

The options are detailed in the table below, and you can use as many or as few of these as you wish. Where the option has a yes/no answer, you use 1 to represent yes and 0 for no. You can combine options by separating them with a comma, like this:

```
window.open('terms.htm', 'termswindow', 'width=500,
height=400,scrollbars=1,status=0,menubar=0,toolbar=0');
```

Take care that you don't restrict people from being able to see all the window's content, especially if they use larger text than you. To help protect their users from bad design, Safari always shows scrollbars, and Safari and Firefox always allow windows to be resized. Firefox always shows the address bar and status bar, too.

Option	What it means
width	Width of the window, in pixels.
height	Height of the window, in pixels.
top	Position relative to top of screen, in pixels.
left	Position relative to left of screen, in pixels.
location	Whether to show the address bar. Several modern browsers always show the address bar. This option can also show back, forward and stop buttons.
toolbar	Whether to display the toolbar. In IE7 and later, this includes the Tools menu and Favorites. In earlier versions and in Firefox it includes back, forward and stop buttons.
menubar	Whether to show the menubar, which has the File, Edit and other menus (where available).
status	Whether to show the status bar at the bottom.
resizable	Whether the user may resize the window.
scrollbars	Whether there are scrollbars shown. Safari overrides this and always shows scrollbars.

Adding random content

You can make your website feel more dynamic by adding some randomly chosen content to it. This could be used to share a random tip or joke, or call attention to random special offers.

To do this, you need to store a list of tips in an array. An array is a set of variables that all have the same name. To tell them apart, they are numbered starting at zero, and the variable name has square brackets after it with the number between them. For example: item[0], item[1], item[2], etc.

Here is some simple JavaScript to put a list of tips into an array, pick one at random and insert it into the web page:

```
function tip_setup()
{
tips=new Array();
tips[0]='First tip goes here';
tips[1]='Second tip here';
tips[2]='Third tip here';
var chosenone=Math.floor(Math.random()*tips.length);
document.getElementById('tip').innerHTML=tips[chosenon
e];
}
```

In your web page, you just need to add an empty <div> section with the id of tip:

```
<div id="tip"></div>
```

The JavaScript will change the content of that div (its innerHTML) to the content of one of the array variables. You also need to trigger the tip_setup() function when the web page loads, by adding an onLoad event to the <body> tag:

```
<body onLoad="tip_setup();">
```

You can easily modify this code to add as many tips as you want. To add another tip, just add another one in the code above:

```
tips[3]="Extra tip here";
```

Each time you add a tip, increase the number in square brackets by one. Each tip should have a unique number, and no numbers should be skipped (so don't go from tips[7] to tips[9], for example). The code will always pick randomly from all the tips you've provided.

Writing Wisdom

I think I did pretty well, considering I started out with nothing but a bunch of blank paper

- Steve Martin

Above: I used some JavaScript similar to this to create the random Writing Wisdom box on my website.

If you want to include an apostrophe in the text of a tip, you have to add a \ before it, so it doesn't get confused with the marker for the end of the tip content.

Use links or any other HTML in your tips. Use CSS to style the content of your #tip box as you would normally.

This slideshow looks most effective when the images are all the same size and orientation.

How does it work? The function newSlide() is given 1 or -1 to add to the slide number when a button is clicked. It adds that number to thisImg, which stores the current slide number. If that makes thisImg 0, it is changed to be the last image number. If it is more than the last image number, it is changed back to 1. The <img> tag is found through its id of slideshow. Its src is changed to be the image number with ".jpg" on the end, so 1.jpg, 2.jpg, and so on.

Adding a photo slideshow

Here's some JavaScript you can use to create a slideshow, which users control by clicking buttons for the next or previous photo in the sequence. You could also use this for displaying pages of a book, or presentation slides from a business slideshow.

1 Collect a set of pictures and give them numbers for names: 1.jpg, 2.jpg, 3.jpg, and so on. The numbers represent the order in the slideshow.

2 Add this HTML where you would like your slideshow to be on the page:

```
<form>
<img src="1.jpg" id="slideshow" alt="Photo slideshow">
<p>
<input type="button" value="<-- Previous photo"
onClick="newSlide(-1)">
<input type="button" value="Next photo -->"
onClick="newSlide(1)">
</p>
</form>
```

3 Add this code between the <head> and </head> tags of your HTML document:

```
<script type="text/javascript" >
thisImg = 1;
imgCt = 10;
function newSlide(direction) {
thisImg = thisImg + direction;
if (thisImg == 0) {thisImg = imgCt;}
if (thisImg == imgCt+1) {thisImg = 1;}
document.getElementById('slideshow').src = thisImg +
'.jpg';
}
</script>
```

4 Change the number in the line imgCt = 10 to be the number of your last photo.

5 Test it to check that all photos are shown and that the buttons work correctly.

Saving time with jQuery

One way you can save time in writing your JavaScript, and ensure that it works across a wide range of browsers, is to use a JavaScript library or framework. This is a collection of often-used JavaScript functions. Using one means that you can focus on designing your site, instead of reinventing the wheel by creating something like a new show/hide routine, a problem that many thousands of developers have already solved before you.

jQuery is one of the most popular libraries at the moment. It makes it easy to create the kinds of visual effects often associated with social networking websites, such as boxes that scroll into view or page elements that fade in and out. It also simplifies a lot of the basic JavaScript and CSS activities you might want to undertake, such as adding content to a page or removing it again.

To get started with jQuery, visit **http://jquery.com** and download the library. There are two versions: the development version might make some sense to you, if you wanted to edit it. The minified version has all the spaces squeezed out, so it's almost impossible to decipher. It's much smaller, though, so that's the version you want to add to your website. To add the library, you use code like this:

```
<script type="text/javascript"
src="jquery-1.10.2.min.js"></script>
```

The numbers in the filename indicate the version number, and the word min shows that it's the minified version.

Your jQuery commands all belong inside a code snippet that checks whether the page is ready first. It looks like this:

```
<script type="text/javascript">
$(document).ready(function()
{
    jQuery code goes here
});
</script>
```

To use jQuery, you can modify the examples from the documentation. Take care with the type and position of brackets, though. I'll show you three quick demonstrations (on the next page) that give some insight into the power of jQuery. It takes some time to get to grips with the syntax of jQuery, but these should show you what can be achieved in a few lines.

Beware

If you only wanted to use a toggle routine, it would be a waste to add 90k of jQuery to your website. It would slow down the site and might impact the user experience. If you're going to use a library, make sure you make the most of it.

Hot tip

You can download the jQuery library from Google's server into your web page. There's a good chance your visitors will already have this version cached in their browser from their visits to other sites that use it. That helps to speed up your site and cuts your server bandwidth. See **https://developers.google.com/speed/libraries/devguide#jquery**

2 quick jQuery examples

Adding a toggle button

You can use jQuery to add a simple show/hide toggle button, but with added sophistication. For example, add your terms like this:

```
<div id="terms">Terms and conditions HTML here</div>
```

You don't want to deny those without JavaScript the ability to see those terms, so this <div> section should be displayed by default. You can then use jQuery to add a button to show or hide the terms above them, and to hide the terms by default. You can use a scrolling visual effect (called "slide" in jQuery) to make the terms and conditions appear to roll up or down. The jQuery code for doing that looks like this:

```
$(document).ready(function()
{
$('<input type="button" value="Show/hide terms"
id="termsbutton">').insertBefore('#terms');
$('#termsbutton').click(function() { $('#terms').
slideToggle(); } );
$('#terms').hide();
});
```

Adding a date picker

The jQuery library is supplemented by jQuery UI (**www.jqueryui.com**), which provides lots of user interface components, such as tabs, input sliders (like a volume control), and progress bars. One of these is the date picker. You need to add the jQuery UI library to your HTML in addition to jQuery, download it and then incorporate it with a <script> tag. Then, if you have a text input tag with an ID of datebox, you can add a date picker using this line of jQuery code:

```
$(document).ready(function()
{
$(function() {$( '#datebox' ).datepicker({}); });
});
```

The only HTML required is:

```
<input type="text" id="datebox">
```

Hot tip

You add a comment in JavaScript the same way you do in CSS:

/*This is a comment*/

If it's just a single line comment, you can put // at the start of the line instead. If you want to "turn off" a line of your JavaScript for testing purposes, you can just put // at the start of it and the browser will ignore it.

Hot tip

You can learn more on jQuery in **jQuery in easy steps**.

9 Audio, video and Flash

Audio, video and animation bring your website to life. One of the most popular tools for all three of these things is Flash.

A piece of content in the Flash format is called a Flash movie.

Beware

Make sure you provide textual alternative content for devices that don't support Flash. That will also help search engines to find and index your Flash content.

Hot tip

The walkthroughs in this chapter were prepared using Adobe Flash Professional CC. If you have a different version of Flash, you might find different snippets or components are available, or are used in slightly different ways.

What is Flash?

Flash is a technology for adding interactive animations and multimedia to web pages. Its influence has reduced in recent years as it's become easier to make sophisticated animations using HTML, CSS and JavaScript. It remains popular for creating online games and adverts, and can also be used for embedding video and audio in a web page.

The strength of Flash is that content you write will run anywhere the plug-in is installed. It means you don't have to worry about the quirks of different browsers, which often require workarounds when using HTML, CSS and JavaScript. The downside of Flash is that it won't run without the plug-in, so it doesn't work on devices that don't support it. That includes the Apple iPhone and iPad, as well as assistive devices such as screenreaders.

Flash is developed and marketed by Adobe. While some third-party tools can be used to create Flash content, most people use Adobe Flash Professional, or other Adobe tools.

You can get a free 30 day trial of Adobe Flash Professional from **www.adobe.com**

Right: Tourism Ireland (**www.tourismireland.com**) created a Flash advert where you can chat to Dara to get his recommendations for places to see in Ireland.

Left: The Coca-Cola Zero website (**http://possible. cokezero.com**) uses Flash for all its content, including this game where you must impress your girlfriend with your drumming skills.

Using Flash Professional

The interface for Flash Professional can be customized in lots of different ways. You can move the panels anywhere you like, and there are different default workspace arrangements available for animators, designers, developers, and small screen users.

Some of the important elements include:

- **Stage.** This is where you create and preview your Flash movie. This is on the left of my workspace, below.

- **Tools.** These are used to draw elements you want to incorporate into your animation, shown in the right pane.

- **Timeline.** The timeline shows you what's happening on the stage and when. Each box on the timeline represents one frame of the animation. The animation can feature many different layers of content, which are combined in the movie. My timeline is below the stage.

- **Library.** Shown to the immediate right of the stage, the library enables you to manage the elements that make up your Flash movie.

- **Menu bar.** Running across the top of the screen is a menu bar that provides access to all the features, and enables you to show or hide different panels.

To open one of the panels, use the Window menu on the menu bar. This also brings a menu to the front if you can't find it.

Hot tip

You can cut the size of your Flash movie by reusing content as much as possible. In my giraffe animation, I created one leaf, and then made a branch that reused that leaf. The eyes and ears were also reused.

Hot tip

An editable Flash file has the extension .fla. When you publish a Flash movie, Flash gives you an HTML file and an SWF file. The HTML file includes the code you need to put the Flash movie into a web page. The SWF is the compressed version of the Flash movie you put on your web server.

Adding video using Flash

The most popular way to add video to a website is to use Flash. Here's how you do that:

1 Start Adobe Media Encoder. This is used to convert your video into the FLV format Flash uses.

2 Your queue of videos to convert is in the top left and should be empty. Drag your video file onto the queue box and drop it there.

3 The video's entry in the queue has several pieces of information. The first one is the target video format. Click it and change it to F4V. This is the latest and highest quality Flash video format. You can also use FLV, an older Flash video format.

Hot tip

Another way to add video to your website is to post it to YouTube (**www.youtube.com**). YouTube takes care of hosting your bulky video file, and gives you code you can paste into your website to show the video there. After you have uploaded your video, go to its page and click the Embed button to get this code. The drawback of using YouTube is that Google adds adverts to your videos. You don't need any additional software, though, and a video that can be easily found on YouTube might attract more viewers and comments than one on your website.

4 Click to open the menu beside your video's second information item (where it says "Match Source Attributes"). Choose the size and quality of your finished video here. If you're not sure which to use, then 320 x 240 or 512 x 218 is usually big enough for comfortable viewing but will fit inside a web page comfortably.

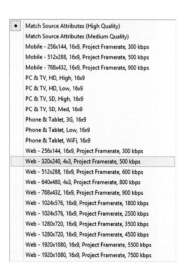

...cont'd

5 Click the output file and use the file browser to choose where you want to save your converted video.

6 Click the Start button, which is a green triangle in the top right of the queue box.

7 Open Adobe Flash Professional and create a new document. Open the Components panel (via the Window menu). In the Video folder, find the FLVPlayback component, click it and drag it onto the stage.

8 Click the video player on the stage and then open its properties (again through the Window menu). Click beside Source to add the name and folder of the FLV file.

9 Click the File menu and then click Publish.

10 You can copy the code in the HTML page that Flash generates into any web page you want the video player to appear in. The finished video player is shown below with its controls for play and pause, volume and mute.

Hot tip

You can change the size of your video player by editing its properties. If you only want to have a video player in this Flash movie and no other Flash content, change the size of the stage so it matches the size of your video player.

Hot tip

HTML5 enables you to add video and audio to your website as easily as you can add an image. The problem is that its use and the file formats are not yet standardized in browsers. For the time being, you need to use Flash, either by itself, or as a fallback option.

163

Adding audio using Flash

You can use Flash to add a simple MP3 player to your website. When somebody presses the button, your MP3 will start playing. When they press again, it will stop. Follow these steps:

Hot tip

There are lots of other form controls in the components panel. You can use these to help standardize your interface, so it's easier to use.

1 In the components panel, find the Button. Click it and drag it onto the stage. In the properties panel, change its label to "Play/Stop music".

2 Open the code snippets panel. Find the snippet to play or stop a sound. Click on your button on the stage, and then double-click on the play sound snippet.

3 The Actions panel opens and shows you the code snippet to play your music, together with instructions at the top. Edit the path and filename for the MP3 file. If it's in the same folder as your Flash file, you can just use its filename (such as "happy.mp3").

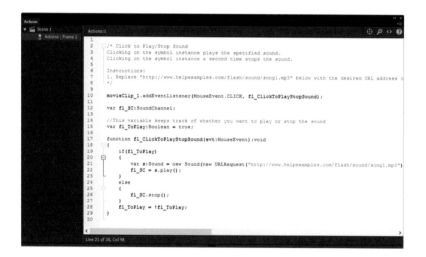

4 To test your Flash movie, use CTRL+Enter. Check that the audio plays and stops when you push the button.

5 Publish your Flash movie, through the File menu. You can copy the code in the HTML file and paste it into any web page you want your music player button to be available in.

Creating a Flash animation

This tutorial introduces the workflow for creating a simple animated scene showing a ship sailing on the ocean. It shows you two ways of animating.

1 Use the rectangle tool to create a box for the sky. In the Color panel, set the line around the box to invisible (a white box with a red line through it), and change the fill color to linear gradient. Click the paint box underneath the horizontal gradient box, and click on red in the color box above. Make the second paint box orange.

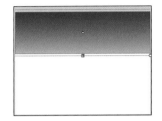

2 Click the gradient transform tool in the Tools panel and then click your sky box. Click the control in the corner and hold it to rotate the gradient angle from vertical to horizontal. Click the control on the line that joins it and hold it to compress or stretch the pattern.

3 Double-click Layer 1 on the timeline and rename it Sky. Click the New Layer button on the timeline. Rename Layer 2 to Sun. Select it and then use the oval tool to add a yellow circle, split by the horizon.

New Layer button

Above: How the sunset scene is built up.

4 Add another layer, and call it Sea. In this layer, create another colored rectangle and give it a gradient fill using two shades of blue. In the timeline, layers that are higher up the screen appear in front of those below, so the sea should hide the bottom half of the sun. You can click and drag layers in the timeline to change their order.

Hot tip

If the gradient transform tool isn't showing, click and hold the Free Transform tool to find it.

...cont'd

Don't forget

Each symbol has its own timeline, separate from the main timeline. You use this to add animation within the symbol, such as flashing lights or spinning radars.

5 Click Insert on the menu and then choose New Symbol. Call it Boat, and make it a movie clip. The stage will clear.

6 Draw your boat. You can use a combination of rectangles, circles, lines and free hand drawing. It doesn't matter how big your boat is. In the document properties, make your stage blue so you can see how your boat will look at sea.

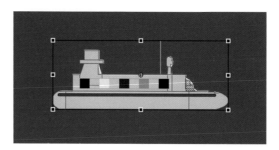

7 On the timeline, right-click in frame 20 and choose Insert Keyframe. A keyframe is a significant frame in the animation.

Make some changes to the version of your boat in frame 20. For example, I widened the radar dish to make it look like it's spinning, and added a red light on top of the pole.

Add a new keyframe at frame 40, but don't make any changes there. This will ensure your boat version from frame 20 displays for another 20 frames, before the animation loops back to the first frame.

Hot tip

A keyframe is shown on the timeline with a black spot in the box. Layers don't all have to have a keyframe at the same point: they can all animate separately.

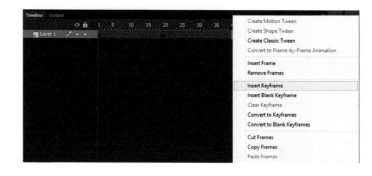

8 Click Scene 1, above the stage, to return to your sunset.

9 Add a new layer and call it Boat. Click this layer on the timeline. In the Library panel, click your Boat symbol and drag it off the left of the stage, at the height of the sea. You can use the Free Transform tool to change its size.

10 Right-click on your boat on the stage, and choose create motion tween. Click on the boat and drag it through the stage and off the other side.

Above: Adding the motion tween. You specify the start and end of the path. Flash automatically generates the intermediate animation frames. I've changed my boat color here for clarity.

167

11 To slow the boat down, click on the keyframe in your boat layer's timeline, which marks the end of the animation. You can then click it and drag it right. To ensure your background also displays throughout, click in the timeline for each layer, and right-click to insert a frame at the end of the animation.

12 Add another layer in the foreground and add flowers and trees to create the impression that you're watching the sea from your balcony. Press CTRL + Enter to preview your animation.

Hot tip

You can add lots of boats in different layers and animate them. You can change their size, color tint, and direction. Flash only needs to put one copy of the Boat symbol into your movie, so there's virtually no impact on file size. The animation (minus the trees) is just 3KB, and it's only 4KB with two boats.

Top tips for Flash animation

1 The best Flash, like the best images, is used to add content and not just decoration. Use Flash to enhance the way visitors can interact with your content and ideas.

2 Take care that your animations don't distract from other important content on the page. Rapid movements can be irritating, and hard for visitors to ignore when they're trying to concentrate on something else.

3 If you do have a Flash introduction (or "intro") on your site, make it stunningly brilliant, and reiterate its themes in the rest of your site. Don't just bolt on special effects at the start and then forget them. Whenever you have full-screen animation, give visitors a Skip button.

4 Take care not to create boxes of Flash content the same shape and size as an advert. People will tend to ignore content they think might be advertising. See Chapter 15 for details of standard advert sizes.

5 Keep an eye on your total file size for the page. If your content takes too long to download, you risk losing visitors who aren't prepared to wait.

6 If you do have a large download, provide a progress meter to show people how long they must wait, and consider providing some simple content to keep them entertained while the real site loads.

7 New versions of the Flash Player are released from time to time. Sometimes Flash movies will only run on the latest player version, but, if you don't require its unique features, try to ensure compatibility with earlier versions. It takes people time to upgrade, so you should ensure your content remains open to as many people as possible.

8 When you use any content requiring a plug-in, always provide good alternative content for those who can't see it.

Beware

Don't let a Flash intro become a frustrating barrier between users and your real content. Visitors are impatient, and many of them will leave rather than sit through an intro.

Above: The Coca-Cola Zero website has a simple helicopter game to play while the main site loads. The progress counter shows how much of the site has downloaded so far.

10 Tools for website design

Using the right tools can save you a lot of time when you design your website.

Using Microsoft Word

You might find that a lot of the content you want to put online is already formatted in a Word document, so you can use Word to create a basic web page. That could save a lot of time marking up content, although you'll still need to edit the resulting HTML and incorporate it into your web design.

Hot tip

If you have images in your document, Word will automatically compress and optimize them for the Web when you save as a web page. They will be saved in a new folder along with your HTML file.

Beware

Word isn't designed to be used for website design, so it's fairly limited. It can't accurately convert text boxes, column layouts, image positions or background images to HTML. Word is best used for marking up your content structure if that content is already in Word. You can then edit the resulting HTML and incorporate it into your web page using your web design tool.

1 Format your document structurally, using the Heading 1 style for your main headline, Heading 2 for your

second level headings, and so on. To apply a style, select the text and then click the style name in the Styles list.

2 Through the Insert tab, you can add a link (called a Hyperlink). To link to somewhere in the same document, insert a Bookmark and give it a name, and then insert a Hyperlink to that Bookmark.

3 Click the File tab (in Word 2010 and 2013) or the Office button (in Word 2007), and click Save As. Change the File type to Web Page, Filtered. You can click Change Title to add some text to go between your <title> and </title> tags. Click the Save button.

4 Open your HTML file in your editor of choice. The CSS instructions are at the top of the document. Your content will be marked up with HTML and will include some Word classes and styles, some of which you might want to edit out. You can now add your content to your website, with the headstart of correctly marked-up text.

HTML and visual editors

There are many simple website editing tools that make web designers more productive. Depending on the tool's focus, it can be described as an HTML editor or a visual editor.

How HTML editors help

HTML editors are like an evolution of the basic text editor, but optimized for creating web pages. They make it easier to create HTML (and CSS) by providing the ability to add tags with a single click, color coding the markup (so the tags can be easily differentiated from the content), and providing simple interfaces to help you to enter meta data or insert images.

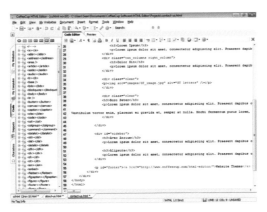

CoffeeCup HTML Editor is an example of one of these tools and costs $69, which is about £43 (*correct at the time of printing*). Its features include:

- **Quick Start.** Type in a web page's title, link colors, background color and/or image, doctype, and meta tags, and the tool will create an empty web page with all that information marked up.

- **Themes.** Off-the-shelf page layouts that you can customize.

- **Code.** A full list of valid tags and their attributes for different versions of HTML. Click one to add it to your page.

- **A table designer.** Enter your table data into the designer, and the editor will add your HTML table formatting.

- **Preview.** See what your website might look like in a browser with a single click.

For designers who like to work with the HTML code, HTML editors make life easier without taking any of the control away.

There is a free trial of CoffeeCup HTML Editor available at **www.coffeecup.com**

HTML editors also provide tools to help your code quality, such as code validators, and cleanup tools that ensure consistent formatting and standardization.

171

One of the most useful features in an HTML editor is the ability to search and replace some text or HTML across all the files of your website. You'll often want to make the same change to all your web pages.

...cont'd

How visual editors help

Visual design tools attempt to hide the complexity of web design by providing a simple graphical interface for designing websites. The advantage is that you don't need to understand HTML to create a web page. You just need to learn how to use the visual tool, which will have features similar to a word processor or art package.

The drawback with using visual tools is that you often can't edit the HTML, so you lose some control, and the underlying code can sometimes be unnecessarily longwinded.

There are two ways you can use visual design software. The first is to install it on your computer to create your website offline, and then upload it to a server in the usual way. CoffeeCup Visual Site Designer is a tool that works like this, and includes a number of templates, complete with color schemes, example navigation, and stock photography.

Alternatively, you can use online services that enable you to build a website, often built and displayed using Flash. Online design tools include Moonfruit (**www.moonfruit.com**), Weebly (**www.weebly.com**), Webs (**www.webs.com**) and Wix (**www.wix. com**). Many hosting companies also provide their own visual editor. These tools can be extremely effective and save any hassle uploading pages. They're also often free. (*Correct at the time of printing.*) But they do tend to lock you in to using a particular company for hosting your site. If you change hosts, you might not be able to use your existing website design any more.

Beware

Some templates can look a bit generic, and, if you use a template, your visitors might already have seen your website design elsewhere. If you want to use a template, choose carefully.

Above: CoffeeCup Visual Site Designer

Left: Moonfruit offers templates, including this one for a photo gallery, and an online tool for customizing them.

Hot tip

You can also buy professional-looking templates you can edit, from sites such as Template Monster (**www.templatemonster. com**). You'll need to understand how to edit the graphics, CSS and HTML files to use them for your site.

Introducing Dreamweaver

Adobe's Dreamweaver is a sophisticated web design package, often used by web design studios to build commercial websites. It's extremely powerful, and enables developers to both edit the code and to use a visual interface to preview the design, edit content, and select content for styling with CSS. Developers can switch seamlessly between the code and the visual views, and an update in one is automatically reflected in the other.

The image below shows the Expanded view, which allocates more room to the menus on the right. The web page that is being designed is on the left. You can click the Code button to see the HTML or CSS in this space instead, or you can view the code and design side by side using the Split view.

On the right, you can see the CSS Designer panel. This shows you all the style rules that are in use. You can edit these properties (such as changing the background color on an element), add new properties to these rules, or add new rules (such as creating a new class of content). As well as writing or editing the CSS syntax yourself, you can use a simple form to define it.

On the right at the top, you can also see the Insert panel, which makes it easy to insert HTML elements in your page.

At the bottom, the properties panel enables you to edit the properties for the item that has been selected in the editing window above, in this case, the large picture.

Hot tip

Although Dreamweaver has a highly visual and menu-driven interface, it is most suitable for people who understand (or are willing to learn) the basics of coding a site in HTML and CSS.

173

Hot tip

Dreamweaver and Flash are part of Adobe Creative Cloud, which licenses Adobe's software on subscription. Prices start at $20 or £18 per month to use one application. The minimum subscription length is 12 months. (*Correct at the time of printing.*) There is a free trial at **www.adobe.com**

A Dreamweaver tour

This walkthrough will give you a flavor of the features and working practices of Dreamweaver, highlighting some of the ways that Dreamweaver makes life easier for web designers.

1 Start by creating a new Dreamweaver Site to keep your Dreamweaver files organized. When you click the New Dreamweaver Site button on the Welcome screen, you are asked to give it a name (which is just for your reference) and a folder location. Click the Save button.

2 Use the File menu to add a new HTML page. You can choose a predefined HTML and CSS template for a two or three column layout. Choose your desired doctype (which will be HTML5 by default) and whether you want your layout CSS in the head of the HTML file, or in a separate new file (which is easier to edit and enables you to share it across the pages on your website). Click the Create button.

3 Your web page is created using the template. The dummy content comprises instructions explaining how the template has been designed.

...cont'd

4 Edit the text in the template. You can use the Properties panel at the bottom of the screen for formatting.

Simplify the interface by closing any panels you don't need.

5 To add an image, position the cursor where you want to add the picture. Open the Insert menu at the top of the screen, and choose Image. Browse to your file, and after it's been added, type the alternative text in the Properties panel. You can also insert a rollover image. You provide two image files, and Dreamweaver will make the picture change when the mouse rolls over it.

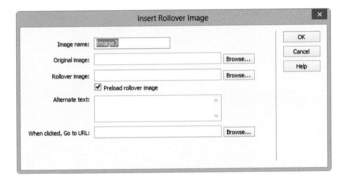

Don't forget you can take a look at the HTML and CSS at any time. Just click the Code button above the editing area.

6 Open the Files panel on the right if necessary so you can see the other files that make up your website. To add a link to another page on your website, highlight the text you would like to turn into a link. In the properties panel at the bottom, click the target icon beside the link box, hold the mouse button down, then point to the file in the Files panel on the right. When you release the mouse button, your link is created. You can also type or paste an address in the Link property box if you want to link to an external website.

You can upload pages to your web server from within Dreamweaver.

175

...cont'd

Position your cursor somewhere, and the Properties panel at the bottom of the screen will show you which CSS rule applies there, and give you quick access to edit it.

Hot tip

In the Site menu is an option to check the internal links across your site. This tool increases your productivity and helps to improve quality.

Hot tip

There are options to clean up your HTML in the Commands menu, including an option to strip unnecessary code from HTML created with Microsoft Word.

7. To edit one of the CSS rules, use the CSS Designer panel. Click the CSS file in the Sources box, and click the rule you'd like to change in the Selectors box. In the Properties box, you can edit the style options without needing to remember any CSS. Your choices are converted to CSS for you and added to your style sheet.

8. You can use Snippets to add commonly used chunks of code. You can create your own, or draw upon the library provided, which includes a text box with placeholder text that disappears, a slideshow, a random image picker, and a breadcrumb trail. Use the Window menu to display the Snippets panel. The Snippets are just pieces of code you paste into your HTML, so make sure you're in Code view before you click Insert at the bottom of the window.

11 Adding a shopping cart

PayPal offers a simple way to add a shopping cart to your website, so it's easy for customers to buy several items in one transaction and pay for them securely.

Essentials for ecommerce

Selling online is often called "ecommerce". If you want to sell online, you need to be able to accept payments through your website. People expect to be able to click the Buy button, enter their credit card and delivery details, then complete their transactions, without the hassle of having to email or enter into a discussion with you. The easier you make it for customers to buy, the more likely they are to do so.

To be able to sell on your website, you need the following:

- **Self-service products.** Typically, this means products that are either standardized or are easy to customize using the website. It's easy to sell books online, but it's much more difficult to sell services, such as building or plumbing services. If there's a level of consultancy involved in making a sale, or delivering a service, your priority should be to get customers to email or phone you, so that you can close the sale personally.

- **Prices declared on your website.** You can't accept payment online if you want to try and sell at different prices to different customers, or want to keep your prices secret.

- **A secure way to collect payment and delivery details.** Data is usually sent over the Internet as text that can be understood by anyone who intercepts the message. Fraudsters can use sniffer programs, which look out for passing data that has the same format as a credit card number or other sensitive information, and then take a copy of it. To avoid sensitive data being intercepted, use a secure connection. This will encrypt communications between the customer's computer and the server, so it's meaningless to anybody who intercepts it.

- **A way to process payments.** If you are already a business that accepts credit cards, your bank should be able to help with this. If you are not already authorized to accept credit card payments, your bank can advise you on the best way to proceed, but banks will want to make sure that your business is proven and trustworthy before giving you a merchant account for accepting card payments.

Many businesses use a payment service provider, which offers a cost-effective way to collect payment information securely, charge the customer's account, and forward the funds to the retailer.

Hot tip

The fees charged by payment service providers vary greatly. Check the fees you will be charged, and make sure they are reflected in the prices you offer to customers.

What is PayPal?

PayPal (**www.paypal.com**) is a payment service provider that enables anyone to send money to anyone else over the Internet. It's often used for settling auction payments and is owned by eBay, the largest online auction site. It can also be used to accept payments on your website, and, because so many people already have a PayPal account, it's often a convenient way for your customers to pay you.

PayPal protects buyers by keeping their payment information secret, and just forwarding the money on to the seller. Buyers can make a payment with a credit or debit card, or using any balance stored in their PayPal account. It is free for buyers to use PayPal, but if PayPal has to convert currencies for them, a fee is built into the exchange rate.

Sellers can keep the money they receive in their PayPal accounts to pay for their own purchases, or they can transfer it to their bank accounts. Sellers are charged a transaction fee of a few percent on each sale. The fees are on a sliding scale and fall as the volume of monthly business increases.

Using PayPal, you can easily accept payments from most countries worldwide, using credit cards or debit cards. Depending on the approach you take, you might not need your own secure hosting, which makes it particularly suitable for websites expecting a smaller volume of online sales. It also provides an inexpensive way of testing the ecommerce market for your business without needing to invest upfront in fees or having to deal with your bank.

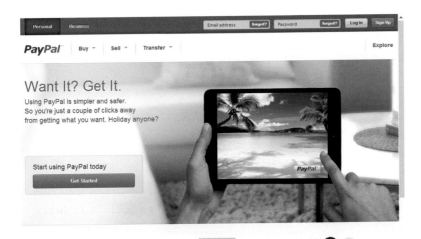

If you're selling digital products, it might be easier to sell your product through Amazon's Kindle for ebooks and Apple's iTunes for music.

179

If you don't want to carry stock, Cafepress (**www.cafepress.com**) and Zazzle (**www.zazzle.com**) enable you to upload a design and have products, such as calendars, mugs and t-shirts, made when customers order them ("on demand" manufacturing). The sites manage payments, manufacturing and shipping, and then pay you a royalty. Lulu (**www.lulu.com**) offers a similar service if you want to publish and sell books.

A shopping cart is a metaphor often used on websites. The shopping cart is just a place where you can store products you intend to buy. You can usually click a button to add something to your shopping cart, and can click on the cart to see the items in it, and/ or remove any. When you "check out", you pay the total price to buy the items in your cart.

British English websites sometimes use the term "shopping basket", instead of "shopping cart". The British term "shopping trolley" is never used online.

Choosing the right cart

There are two different ways you can use PayPal to implement a shopping cart on your website.

The most advanced method is to use shopping cart software that integrates with PayPal. Some of this, including OS Commerce (**www.oscommerce.com**) and Zen Cart (**www.zen-cart.com**), is free and open source (which means you can see and adapt the code that runs it). These shopping carts are a particularly good solution if you intend to sell a large number of different products. They work using a database, so you don't have to worry about adding payment buttons to lots of different web pages.

To use a shopping cart like this, you will need to use a hosting company that supports PHP and MySQL. Installation is a complex process, but some hosting companies offer a pre-installed shopping cart with their business hosting packages. PayPal publishes a list of partners that offer shopping cart services.

If you intend to sell digital products (such as ebooks or music), you should use a shopping cart that enables immediate download of the product once the payment is validated.

PayPal also provides tools that you can use to create buttons for your website in HTML. They are simple to use, and don't require any software installation. Although you can pay a monthly fee for a PayPal Payments Pro account, so you can accept payments on your own website, there is also a Standard account that has no monthly fee and enables you to direct customers to the PayPal site to complete their transaction. In this chapter, I'll show you how to create a simple shopping cart using PayPal's tools.

Creating your cart buttons

In this walkthrough, I'll show you how to create a simple shopping cart using the PayPal Button Factory. You need to create a different Add to Cart button for each product you will sell.

1 Log in to your PayPal account. If you don't already have a PayPal account, visit **www.paypal.com** and register for a business account.

2 Go to the PayPal Button Factory at **https://www.paypal.com/buttonfactory** It's shown below.

3 Change the button type to Shopping Cart.

If you're selling a handful of products, this is the ideal approach. If you have lots of products, using a database-driven cart will save you a lot of time and effort.

If you only have one product, you don't need a shopping cart. You can change Step 3 to the button type of a Buy Now button. You won't need to add a View Cart button, but otherwise the process is similar to the one here.

...cont'd

4 Type the item name into the box. You can also give it a unique ID number to make it easier to track sales.

5 Enter the price and currency into the box.

6 Alternatively, you can add a dropdown menu with different prices and options. This is for choosing variants of this product and should not be used for choosing different products. I've used it for selling a photographic print in different sizes, for example.

7 If the choices have no bearing on the price, add a dropdown menu without prices instead. You might use this to let customers pick the color of a shirt, for example. You can use the two different option dropdowns together (use one for size, one for color, for example).

8 You can customize the button with your own image, but the PayPal image is widely recognized, so the default might encourage customers to use it.

9 Set the postage amount.

10 Make sure you choose to use your secure merchant account ID. This will stop your email address being published in your web page for spammers to harvest.

Beware

PayPal has a timeout on it. If you don't finish creating your buttons quickly enough, your session will be cancelled. You can keep your session going by clicking Continue when the warning appears.

Beware

Websites sometimes change how they are designed, and how they work. The process is slightly different in the US and UK. Your experience might differ from that described here.

11 Click the blue Step 2 bar if you want to add inventory tracking. You can tell PayPal the stock levels of your product and it will alert you when you're running out. You can also tell it how much your items cost, and it will help you to track your profit and loss.

Hot tip

PayPal also has buttons for accepting donations and regular subscription payments.

12 Click the blue Step 3 bar for advanced options. From here, you can choose to direct customers to a thank you page on your website after a sale, or a "can we help you?" page if the sale is abandoned.

Don't forget

You don't need any special hosting requirements, nor any special software, to use this shopping cart. It will work with any website, and PayPal takes care of the secure connection for you. Try it!

13 Click Create Button at the bottom of the form.

Create Button

Beware

Although it might look like a single form on your website, each button has its own <form> and </form> tags in the HTML.

Hot tip

It doesn't matter whether your products and their Add to Cart buttons are all on the same page, or whether products appear on different pages throughout your website.

Beware

If you have multiple buttons on the same page, make sure it's obvious which products they belong to.

Adding your cart buttons

PayPal will now give you the HTML code you need to add to your website, so that you can incorporate an Add to Cart button. You will need to know how to edit the HTML of your website to use this (see Chapter 6).

1 Use the preview of your button on the right to check that the dropdown menus (if any) contain the correct information. If not, click the link to edit the button.

2 Click the Select Code button. Right-click on the highlighted HTML code and choose Copy.

3 Open your web page in your HTML editor and paste in the code from PayPal. You should position it so that it appears next to the product information on screen. This bit is fiddly and might take some time. If you use dropdown menus, PayPal will use a table in its code to lay them out. You can delete all the tags related to tables, and it won't interfere with the code working.

4 On the PayPal site, click the link to create a similar button. You can then edit the settings for the previous product to create the next button. Note that you can't just reuse the same code for different products. It looks the same on the screen, but the PayPal HTML code includes information about the product being ordered and its price.

Adding a View Cart button

You also need to add a View Cart button, so your customers can see what they've put in their shopping cart and check out.

1 Once you create an Add to Cart button, one option under it is to create a View Cart button. Click it.

2 You can choose to change the size of the button, or can use your own button image. The advantage of using the PayPal button is that visitors will recognize it from other websites, and its style will match PayPal's default Add to Cart buttons. If you choose to specify your own image, make sure it's intuitive. Consider using a picture of a shopping cart on it.

3 Click Create Button and you'll be given some code to add to your website, as you did for the Add to Cart button.

4 Add this code to your website. While your Add to Cart buttons will appear only on pages where you're selling your products, the View Cart button should be available from any web page. People might put something in their shopping cart and then read some of your articles. If they can't find the View Cart button, they can't pay you. Consider making the button part of your navbar, or putting it in the top right of every page.

Hot tip

When you go to the Button Factory, underneath the menu to choose a button type, there is an option to see your saved buttons, so you can use a previous button as a starting point for a new button.

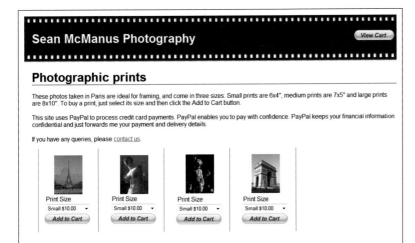

Sean McManus Photography   View Cart

Photographic prints

These photos taken in Paris are ideal for framing, and come in three sizes. Small prints are 6x4", medium prints are 7x5" and large prints are 8x10". To buy a print, just select its size and then click the Add to Cart button.

This site uses PayPal to process credit card payments. PayPal enables you to pay with confidence. PayPal keeps your financial information confidential and just forwards me your payment and delivery details.

If you have any queries, please contact us.

Print Size	Print Size	Print Size	Print Size
Small $10.00 ▼	Small $10.00 ▼	Small $10.00 ▼	Small $10.00 ▼
Add to Cart	Add to Cart	Add to Cart	Add to Cart

The screenshot shows how a simple, one-page website can be made to sell four products, with a prominent View Cart button.

However you integrate ecommerce with your website, it is essential to test that it works correctly. These testing tips will work if you followed the walkthrough in this chapter to add your cart, but the key is to test enough to have confidence that all the buttons work as they should.

Testing your shopping cart

After you've installed your cart buttons, the most important step is to test your shopping cart. The cart itself is pretty reliable, so what you're really testing is that it's installed well on your website. You can do this before you publish your web pages to the Internet, to minimize the risk to real customers. Simply open the web page file on your hard disk in your browser.

Testing can help you to identify any technical problems with your shopping cart. To find out whether it's easy to use, get a friend to test it for you, too.

1 Click one of your Add to Cart buttons. A new PayPal window will open, showing that the item has been added to your shopping cart. Check the prices (including delivery) are correct.

2 Close that window. Try each of the other products in turn to make sure they go into the cart with the correct product name and price. Try choosing different product options, where available.

3 Use the View Cart button to open the shopping cart again. Many users will close pop-up windows they don't need, so it is essential they can easily open the cart again.

4 The process is all under PayPal's control from there on in. If you want to see how it works, ask a friend to buy something from you. You can refund the payment later. You can't use your own account to buy from your own shopping cart.

12 Adding a social dimension

Forums and comments help increase visitor engagement with your website. Integrate with social networks, and visitors might recommend your site, too.

Hot tip

You can get an easy-to-install forum from Bravenet (www.bravenet.com). All the software runs on Bravenet's servers, so you just need to paste a line of JavaScript into your website. There is a free version with adverts, and an affordable paid version that's ad-free.

Hot tip

Enabling discussions and link sharing is a great way to find out what your visitors are most interested in. Make sure you listen to the feedback they give you.

Why social matters

Over the last few years, the social dimension of the web has become increasingly important. The rise of social networking websites, such as Facebook, Twitter and photo sharing site Flickr, has had two important effects:

1. People increasingly discover the websites they visit through personal recommendations from their friends and family in social networking websites. The easier you can make it for people to recommend your website to their social circle online, the more likely they are to do so.

2. The boundaries of the typical website have extended, and it now has tendrils in social networks. Flickr can be an easier way to publish photos and get feedback on them than by incorporating a gallery in your website, for example. Twitter might be the easiest way to share brief news stories and interact with your website visitors. Many website owners will see their site as a hub at the center of their online presence, but will actively publish content on other websites, too.

The effect of social proof can be valuable, too: if someone tells you that 2,000 people like a website, you're bound to spend a moment checking it out. Social networks can keep tabs on how many people recommend your site, which means you can use these statistics to persuade people to take your site seriously. Of course, if only three people have recommended your site, so far, you might want to keep quiet about that number for now.

How much social interaction you allow on your website is up to you, but many websites find that they can be most valuable to their community of visitors by enabling them to interact with each other. People are also more likely to be loyal to other people who frequent a website, than they are to its content (unless it's truly awesome, which I'm sure yours is).

There are several ways you can enable people to socialize on your website. Blog platforms and many content management systems will enable you to accept comments on your content from readers. You can also add a discussion forum easily. phpBB is a free and open source forum that you can incorporate in your website. It's a PHP script, so you'll need a hosting package that supports PHP.

Integrating with Facebook

Facebook is by far the largest social network, and, for many people, it's their number one online destination. Facebook offers a number of what it calls "social plug-ins". These include:

- **Like Button.** A simple button which visitors can click to recommend your site to their Facebook friends. The plug-in can also display how many people have recommended your web page.

- **Recommendations.** A box of links on your website, compiled from the pages that others have recommended. This can be a nice piece of additional exploratory navigation.

- **Activity feed.** This box will show visitors what their friends have recommended on the site recently, and fill the gaps with generic recommendations. Works well for sites that have lots of visitors and sharing activity (such as a newspaper), but is less effective on smaller sites.

To configure any of these, follow these steps:

1 Visit **https://developers.facebook.com/docs/plugins** Pick the plug-in you want to use on the left.

2 Complete the form with your domain name, and edit the appearance settings. Under the form, you'll see a preview of your plug-in. Click Get Code.

3 There are two parts to the code: put the first one just after the <body> tag in your web page. The other goes where you would like your plug-in to appear in the web page.

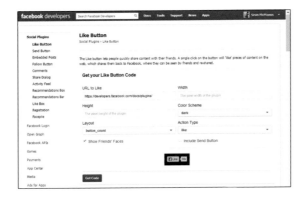

Hot tip

There are also plug-ins to enable comments on your web pages and to embed posts from Facebook into your website.

Hot tip

Facebook can tell you how many people have recommended your site, and their gender, age, and country of origin. Go to **www.facebook. com/insights**

You can also use Twitter to keep past visitors updated and to attract new visitors, by participating in the Twitter community. Encourage site visitors to follow you, and announce new content with a tweet and a link back to your site.

You can embed your latest tweets in your website, too, using a widget like the one below. Visit **https://twitter.com/settings/widgets** to customize the size, color schemes and content. You'll be given some JavaScript code to paste into your website.

Integrating with Twitter

Twitter is a social networking website that enables you to share messages of up to 140 characters with people who choose to follow you. Each message is called a tweet. Members often discover much of the content they read online through Twitter, so it's a good idea to make it easy for people to tweet about your site.

1 Open your web browser and go to **https://twitter.com/about/resources/buttons** Choose the Share a Link button.

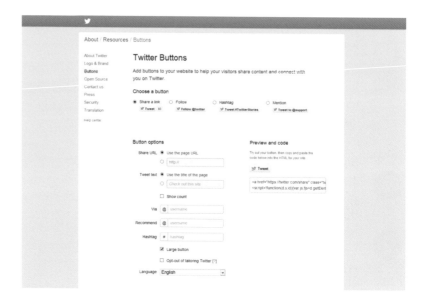

2 By default, the button will tweet the page title and the link of the page the button was on, but you can use the Share URL and Tweet Text options to change those.

3 Enter your username in the Via box, and it will be included in the tweet.

4 After the tweet has been sent, Twitter can recommend that people follow you. Add your username into the Recommend box to enable that.

5 Copy the code provided and paste it into your web page, somewhere where visitors will easily spot it.

Adding a "Share this" box

You can add buttons for all the different social networks individually, but there are a number of different services that enable you to add buttons for the most popular networks (including Twitter, Facebook, Google+ and Pinterest) in one go. Here's how to do that, using Addthis.com:

1 Go to **www.addthis.com** in your web browser and click the Get the Code link on the navbar. Click Share Buttons.

2 There are options for WordPress, Blogger and some other publishing platforms. If it's going into your website, just leave the Website radio button selected.

3 Choose which layout of buttons you'd like to use. If you choose a layout of equally sized icons, Addthis shows each visitor the buttons they are most likely to use.

4 Sign in or create an account if you'd like to enable analytics. This will tell you how many people are sharing your content. The analytics data could be used to refine the placement of your Share buttons. If you don't want to register, click the link to say you don't want analytics.

5 Copy the code provided and insert it in the appropriate place in your web page HTML.

6 Try the button on a couple of different pages on your site to test it works and refers people to the correct page.

Above: Visitors can click the Share button to find a wide range of other social networks and services to share your web page on.

Hot tip

Addthis also offers Follow buttons you can easily customize to encourage visitors to subscribe to your updates on Twitter, Facebook, LinkedIn, Youtube and other social networks and blog platforms.

Adding photos from Flickr

If you use Yahoo's photo sharing website Flickr (**www.flickr.com**), you can add a badge, which displays up to 10 of your photos from Flickr on your site. Your site visitors can click through to Flickr to browse more of your photos, and to add their comments. Adding your Flickr badge to your website is a good way to build a relationship with Flickr members.

If you only want to show some of your Flickr photos on your website, you could create a tag called "forwebsite" and set the badge to only display photos with that tag.

1 If you are not already a member of Flickr, sign up and upload some photos. A basic account is free, and you can use an existing Yahoo ID to register.

2 In your browser, visit h**ttp://www.flickr.com/badge.gne** You'll need to log in. Choose the HTML badge.

3 Choose the content you'd like to use. You can choose to only show content from one set or with a particular tag.

4 Define your layout, including how many photos to display, which size they should be, and which orientation the box should be (vertical or horizontal).

5 Choose colors that will work well with your website.

Flickr can be a great way to publish photos, and has an easy way to upload them. Before creating a photo gallery on your website, which might involve quite a bit of web design work, consider whether you can use Flickr and add a badge to your site to bring people to your photostream.

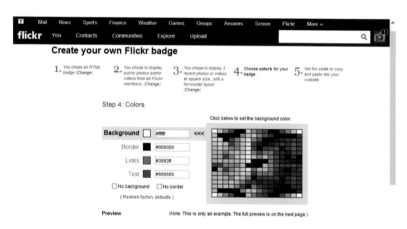

6 Copy the code provided and paste it into your website.

Adding comments

Disqus enables you to accept comments on your website and present them as a discussion.

1 Visit **www.disqus.com** and click Add Disqus to Your Site.

2 Fill out the form to set up your website. You'll need to provide your website address (just your domain name, not the full URL for the page) and create an account.

3 Disqus provides instructions for installation on sites powered by various blogging platforms and content management systems.

4 If you're not using one of these, choose the Universal Code installation option. That gives you some HTML and JavaScript you can paste into any website.

5 Place the HTML code provided where you would like your comments facility to appear in your web page.

6 Test your comments thread works by leaving comments on your own web page. You can always delete them again later.

Disqus is extremely easy to set up: you don't need to have PHP or any other special hosting requirements. You can add a discussion thread to any page of your site. Give it a go!

Blogging software enables you to publish content, solicit comments, and manage them. See Chapter 13.

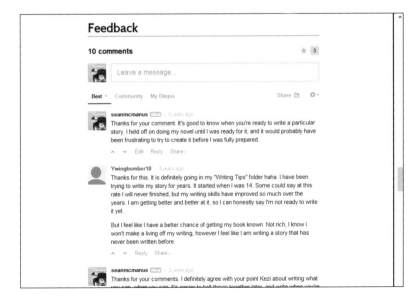

Above: Platforms supported by Disqus.

Left: How the Disqus discussion thread looks in a website.

Moderating comments

If you allow people to publish messages on your website, you should keep an eye on what they write. Unfortunately, there is a small group of extremely prolific spammers who abuse forums and comment facilities to promote their links. Sometimes they will leave vague messages that don't refer to your content and add nothing to the conversation, such as "Great article! Keep up the good work!". Other times, they'll post utter nonsense. You should weed these junk comments out, so that the real discussion can take place without getting bogged down in them.

When you vet comments before allowing them to be published, it's called moderating them. By default, Disqus comments are not moderated before being posted. You can change that by logging into your Disqus account and going to the Settings tab. You can find comments to moderate by clicking the Comments tab.

Blogging platforms, such as WordPress and Blogger, also enable you to moderate comments before they go live.

You should moderate with a light touch: as the site owner, you have the right to decide what is published on the site. But the expectation is that, if you invite people to leave comments, you'll publish anything reasonable, even if you disagree with it. In that case, you can reply to the comment. It undermines the concept of the comments and the forum if you stifle a conversation purely because you disagree with it.

Right: The Disqus website enables you to review and approve the comments your pages receive before they are published on your website.

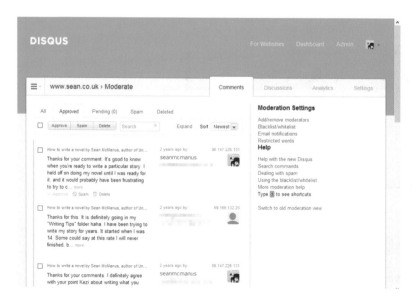

13 Content management systems

Content management systems make it easier to create and manage sites with lots of content or contributors.

What is a CMS?

A content management system (CMS) enables people to create, edit, publish, and manage the content on a website, without needing technical knowledge. It helps in several ways:

Hot tip

Popular content management systems include Drupal (www. drupal.org) and Joomla (www.joomla.org).

- Writers can focus on writing, without having to worry about HTML or any of the technical aspects of adding content to the website. They can style the content using a simple interface that looks and feels similar to a word processor.

- The CMS can automatically add navigation to new content. For example, if you post a new story, the CMS can add a link to your homepage and to related articles.

- You can upload images and other content using a simple web-based interface.

- You can update the site more quickly. All you need to do is write the new content in a web form (or paste it in), and press the publish button. You don't have to design HTML files or upload them to the server yourself.

- You can edit the site from anywhere. You access your content management system over the web, so you can use it from anywhere in the world where you can get a web connection.

- The CMS enforces consistency in the design, because pages (typically) use the same template. You can easily make site-wide changes to your design by changing the template.

- A CMS will often include the ability to accept comments from site visitors, and give you tools to moderate them.

- You can usually enable different people to have access to the system, with different permissions. Some people might be allowed to edit and delete others' content, for example, while more junior team members can only add their own stories.

You can use a CMS to build your whole website, or could use it just to manage parts of it, such as the news section or the blog.

A CMS might not be appropriate for highly visual sites, or sites with a lot of variation in content or design between different pages or sections. Content management systems most help sites with a lot of textual content that use a standardized design across the site.

What is WordPress?

Blogs use a simple content management system. They enable anyone to publish content, which is organized by date. Each article is called a blog post. Supplementary navigation can sort posts into different categories, but the underlying principle is that the content is sorted by date, like an online diary or news feed.

WordPress is a blogging platform, but its sophisticated customization options mean that many people use it to build complete websites. As well as adding blog posts, you can add pages that go onto your navbar. You can organize a hierarchy of pages, too, so you can create subsections of pages inside a main section, enabling you to build a sophisticated site structure.

There are two different versions of WordPress:

1 **WordPress.com.** This is a service that WordPress will host for you. You can quickly and easily set it up, but your customization options are limited, with about 200 themes (or layouts) to choose from. Setting up a basic site is free, but you'll need to pay to edit your CSS or to remove adverts. You can get a free yoursite.wordpress.com address but I recommend you buy a real domain name.

2 **WordPress.org.** This offers PHP software that you need to install on your server. There are over 1,000 themes available, and you have full access to customize them. This is the approach I'd recommend if you want to have control over your website design.

You can use a blog to publish news stories, regular opinion columns, a photo a day, or pretty much anything else.

Alternative blogging systems include Movable Type (www. movabletype.com) and Blogger (www.blogger. com), which is owned by Google.

Left: Author Siobhan Curham (www. siobhancurham.co.uk) manages her website using WordPress.

Setting up WordPress

I'll show you how you can work with WordPress.org, although there are a lot of similarities between the two versions. Everything on these first two pages applies to WordPress.org only, though.

1 Install WordPress. Many hosting companies offer WordPress hosting, with the installation done for you. If you want to use WordPress, the easiest solution is to choose one of these hosting companies. Mine just asked me which folder I wanted WordPress installed in, and asked me for a username and password, and a blog title.

2 Log in. When WordPress has been set up, you should see a default template when you visit your website. It will differ from mine here. Click the link to Log in and enter your username and password.

3 On your Dashboard, click Appearance on the left, and then click Install Themes. You can search using a keyword (e.g. "music"), and specify the features of your template, such as whether it's fixed or flexible width, and how many columns it has.

Hot tip

When you're logged in to WordPress, you'll see your blog title in the top left of the screen. You can click it to visit your public-facing website.

Hot tip

To change your website's title and/or tagline, log in to WordPress and click Settings.

4 Click a theme to preview it. When you've found one you like, click the link to install it. This downloads it into your WordPress CMS, but it doesn't change your website's appearance. To start using a theme, click Appearance on the left, then click Themes. You can see all your installed themes, including small pictures of them. Activate one to start using it on your live website.

The page templates in WordPress are coded using PHP. It's best to learn the basics of PHP syntax before making significant changes, to ensure you don't introduce bugs. But, if you're adept at HTML, you should be able to make minor edits without a problem.

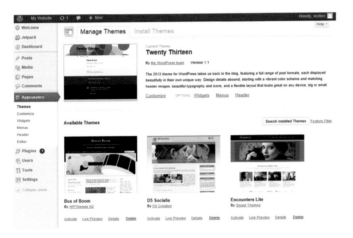

5 To customize your theme, click Customize on the left under Appearance. Different templates will show you different options here. There is a link under Appearance to Menus, which enables you to create a custom menu.

6 Click Editor (under Appearance on the left) and you can edit the CSS and PHP templates.

Visit your public website, and then use your browser's menu to save the complete web page. This will save the HTML, images and CSS to your computer. You can then experiment with editing the CSS using your tool of choice. You can preview the results on your saved page, too. When you're ready, copy and paste the CSS into WordPress.

Adding pages

WordPress lets you add pages to your website. Typically, these pages contain information that will be updated relatively infrequently, such as the About Us section. Pages are added to your navbar.

Above: The navbar on the website shows the pages that have been added to it. The pages Contact Us and Terms and Conditions have the About Us page as their parent, and so appear in a pop-up menu under that section. Use the Order number option when you edit your page to change the order of the links on the navbar.

200

Hot tip

When using the visual editor, you can type in your text and format it using the controls along the top to add bullets and emphasis, and to align the paragraphs. You can also add an image, video or MP3 by clicking Add Media above the content box.

1 Log in to WordPress and click Pages on the left. By default, you have a Sample page. You can see any other pages you have added here, and can click a page title to edit that page. Click the Add New button.

2 Enter your page title in the first box, where it says Enter Title Here. This will be used as the title of the link to this page from the navbar, so keep it short and meaningful. For example: About Us, The Team, Our Offices.

3 Enter the page content in the large box in the middle. You can use a simple visual editor, or you can edit the HTML using the Text tab.

4 You can make a page appear underneath another page in the navigation. For example, you might add Visit Us under About Us. To specify which page you would like the page you're editing to be under, give it a parent in the Page Attributes box on the right.

5 To save your page, click Save Draft on the right. Click the button to Preview your page. When you're happy, click the Publish or Update button.

Adding posts

Posts are typically used for content you intend to update regularly. For example, each news story or new blog entry will be a post. Individual posts aren't added to the navbar, but posts are dated and visitors can browse them by month or post category.

There are similarities in the way that you manage pages and posts, but there are some differences, too. Here's how to add a post:

1 Log in to WordPress and click Posts on the left. You'll see a list of posts and, as with pages, you can edit a post by clicking its title. Click Add New to create a new post.

2 The title won't be used on the navbar, so you can afford to make it more descriptive.

3 Add your content in the same way as you do for pages, in the large box in the middle.

4 On the right, you can add categories for your posts. This is an important navigational tool because it organizes posts into groups people can easily browse. A post can appear in more than one category. For optimal usability, limit your site to a small selection of categories.

5 Add tags to your posts. These are short descriptive keywords or phrases used by visitors to find related posts. Tag classification is looser than a category. An article might be in the "dogs" category if it's all about dogs. It might have the tag "dogs" even if they are just mentioned in passing.

6 You can save a draft while you work. When you've finished, click the Preview button to proofread your post before it's published to the world.

7 Click Publish when it's ready. WordPress will make it the first post on your site, and add it to your archives, category, and tag navigation automatically.

Hot tip

To edit the HTML for your content, click the Text tab along the top of the content box.

Tag cloud

atom C cilk competition concurrency Ct Technology data races debugging develop 2010 DevMob 2010 **game development** gaming Google Haskell

Above: a tag cloud in the sidebar of a WordPress blog. The larger the word, the greater the number of posts that carry that tag. You can add a tag cloud or category listing by clicking Appearance and then Widgets.

Managing comments

WordPress enables you to accept comments on your posts and pages, which can be a valuable way to get feedback from your audience. You need to moderate your posts (see Chapter 12) to ensure your discussion doesn't get bogged down in spam.

1 When you log in to your WordPress site admin system (or Dashboard), you'll be shown how many comments are pending approval. Click Pending to review them.

2 Read the comments. When you hover the mouse over a comment, links will appear to approve the comment or move it to the spam or trash folders. You can use these links to approve or delete comments, if you only have a few. You can also edit comments, although that's rarely used. If you do edit someone's comment, make clear what you've edited, so you don't misrepresent them.

3 If you have lots of comments to process, tick the box beside any you want to approve. Then click the Bulk Actions dropdown menu and choose Approve. Click Apply to approve all ticked comments. Use a similar process (with a different bulk action) to move a group of comments to spam or trash.

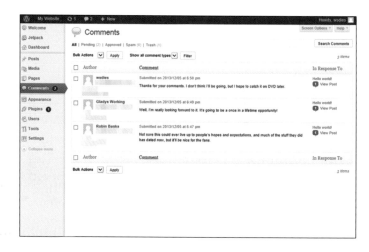

Hot tip

People expect permission to leave comments on posts (which are typically led by opinion or news), but not on pages (which are usually about you). It's probably not appropriate to invite public comments on your terms and conditions, for example. When editing a page or post, scroll down and you can disable or enable comments on it.

Hot tip

Check the spam folder from time to time, in case WordPress has classified a genuine comment as junk by mistake.

14 Testing and launching

Once your site has been designed, you need to test that it works as expected and is easy to use before you publish it on your server.

After spending perhaps months building a site, you might be impatient to launch it. Make sure you plan enough time to test properly before your launch, though. First impressions count.

Hot tip

Websites sometimes do a beta launch, which means they invite people to use the site, on the understanding that there might be the odd bug because it's not yet complete. You can get away with this if your website is innovatively interactive. If you're just publishing content or using well-tried methods of interaction (such as visitor reviews and comments), this smacks of a lack of testing and/ or confidence.

When is it ready to launch?

Building a successful website is rarely a one-off construction job. If it's a business site, you'll want to extend it with new products and services as the business develops. If it's a personal site, you'll want to add new stories, photos, or music.

The beauty of the web is that it's easy to do that, but the downside is that you can get paralyzed into never launching the site, because there's always more you can do. A website that's still on your hard drive isn't really a website at all, so it's a good idea to launch early and expand it gradually, over time. There are five benefits to doing that:

- Google likes to see sites that are growing with new content. If you publish everything at one time, it will think your site is stagnant, and will prioritize more lively sites over yours.

- Search engines can start to index the early content you post, and other sites can start linking to it, so you can begin to build a rank in the search engines. This can take a long time (measured in months), so the earlier you start, the better.

- People won't spend an hour browsing your site to read everything there on their first visit, but you might convince them to visit regularly, to see the new content you've added since their last visit.

- You can refine the design of the site using feedback from visitors and analytics data.

- Whether you want your site to drive sales or build a reputation, the earlier it's live, the earlier it can start working for you.

The one caveat is that the site must offer a complete experience, even if it has fewer features than you ultimately plan to launch. Visitors get frustrated if they click on a link, wait for a web page to download, and then find that it just says "under construction" or, worse still, that the link is broken. Website visitors are impatient and if you waste their time, they'll abandon your site and won't come back. If you haven't created a section yet, don't implement links to it yet, either. You can change any web page any time, so you can always go back and add those links later.

Before launching your site, you should test it thoroughly.

Testing your website

Testing is an important part of the website development process. If you're working with a web design firm, they might send you sections of the website to test at regular intervals. If you're building the site yourself, you'll probably develop the site iteratively, coding something, trying it in your browser, refining your design and repeating, until it's finished.

Before you launch your website, there are two different types of testing you need to perform:

- **Technical testing:** this tests whether the site works as designed. It identifies issues such as broken links and designs that do not render correctly in a particular web browser.

- **Usability testing:** this is about making sure that your site is designed intuitively, so that it can be easily used.

For the best results, you should test your site early during development and test it often. Technical problems tend to be easier to fix the earlier they are identified. To fix a usability problem, you might need to redesign elements of the site or its content. If that's left to the end of the process, you'll already be too committed to the existing design, which will make it harder to justify the delay and expense caused by rework.

Testing your site offline

Most websites can be tested on a computer without uploading them to the Internet. Just open the homepage in your web browser and you should be able to navigate the site. This will only work if your website does not use programs on the server, such as PHP scripts or WordPress.

You will need to reference all files in your HTML using relative paths so that they work on your hard disk. Instead of embedding the image **http://www.example.com/photos/dog.jpg**, for example, use a relative path like photos/dog.jpg. HTML editors can often help you work out the relative path.

You can also upload your website to the Internet at a secret location (often called a staging server). Sometimes it's as simple as creating a folder on your website's intended final server and putting all your files in there. Instead of **www.example.com**, you could test your site running by publishing it at **www.example.com/hidden/ index.htm** and then visiting that page in your browser.

Testing on your computer won't pick up any problems with uploading the website to the server. A common problem is case sensitivity. On your desktop, index.htm and INDEX.HTM are the same file. On the server, they might be treated as two different ones. Make sure you test your website after it goes live, too.

205

Putting your website into a folder you don't tell anyone about gives you some privacy, but if the test version must remain secret, you need to protect your staging server with a password. That will stop search engines stumbling across it and sending it visitors.

Technical testing

Nearly everything you need to know about technical testing is encapsulated in this short guideline: try to break your website. Do anything a visitor might, and anything else you can imagine, that might lead to unpredictable results. Be inventive. For example:

- What happens if you type nonsense into the contact form, register with an invalid email address, or submit incomplete data? Do you end up with corrupt data in your database? Also, can the form cope with foreign addresses?

- What happens if JavaScript or Flash is disabled? Can people still navigate your site and access its core content?

- Does it work on an iPad or games console? What about older desktop browsers? And current versions of Internet Explorer, Firefox, Safari, Chrome and Opera?

- Is the site fast enough when running from a server? What about if you're using a mobile device?

- Do all the links and buttons work as they should? Does the navbar look right in every section of your website?

- Can you discover any broken images?

- Does the forum work as it should? Can you add new posts and reply to others? What about the shopping cart? Or social networking integration? Or email newsletter subscribe box?

Good testing is hard to do. It's easy to just confirm your belief that the website is working, by entering an email address with no @ symbol to check an error message is shown. Or to enter a valid email address to confirm that it is accepted without triggering any alerts. The difficult bit is to test for what happens if the address is invalid in a way you haven't checked for in your validation code (such as a mistyped domain extension).

The goal of technical testing is not to create a perfect website (whatever that might mean). It is to give you confidence that there are no errors in how your site has been coded or configured, and that users don't have a bad experience because of technical issues, or when they make a mistake. Fix important problems, but don't get bogged down in creating an error message and response for every possible mistake. The important thing is that users can find their way back to your homepage if something goes wrong.

Generic Company Marketing Site

Thank you for your response. Your input is appreciated.

Above: I saw this message when I contacted a major music retailer. It told me that they hadn't configured their plug-in contact form from the generic message, and that nobody had ever tested that the script actually worked. I wondered what else they hadn't tested...

Usability testing

In a usability test, you ask people who aren't familiar with the website to try to use it. Here are some top tips:

1 It's best to test with people who are potential users of the website, if you can find them, but it's better to test with anyone than with nobody. Ask a friend or a colleague to give it a go. Anyone who doesn't know the site is fine.

2 Give people a task to do that matches one of the site's goals. For example, ask them to find something they want and buy it on the site. If you can give people some choice in the task, they'll be more emotionally invested in it.

3 While the test is going on, try to stay silent as much as possible. Don't tell people where the buttons are, because the idea is to see how easily they can figure it out. Don't give them too much information about the site beforehand, either. What matters is what's on screen.

4 Don't worry if the user makes a mistake, such as going to the wrong section, and is able to correct that themselves. If they can get themselves back on track, it shows the website is working.

5 You can ask the test participant to tell you about what they're doing while they do it, which might help you to understand their reasoning, and how they feel about the website when they encounter problems.

6 Prioritize those problems that are identified by several different people. You can't please everyone, so don't try to do everything that your participants suggest. In particular, bear in mind that everyone has a favorite color.

7 Test early and often. Ask people, informally, what they think of your sketches. Show them your design mock-ups and ask them to try your unstyled HTML pages, to see if the layout makes sense. If you leave all your testing to the end, it will be too late to make some key changes.

Don't forget

If test participants can't complete a task, they're not stupid. If they can't use your website, you need to refine its design.

Hot tip

After the site goes live, solicit and use feedback from your site visitors, too.

Hot tip

Large organizations invest heavily in usability testing, including using labs with one-way glass, so all the developers can watch the tests take place without scaring the participant. Otherwise, a low-cost informal test over a few sandwiches at lunchtime can still give you amazing insight.

Publishing your site by FTP

To launch your website, you need to copy the files from your computer to the hosting company's server. The method used to do this is called file transfer protocol (FTP). You need to know your FTP server address, your username, and your password. Your hosting company can tell you these.

You can use Windows Explorer (in Windows Vista and later versions) for FTP transfer. This is the process in Windows 8, but it is similar in other versions of Windows too:

Hot tip

If you use a content management system, it will publish pages to your server automatically once you've set it up.

1 Open a Windows Explorer window. You can do that by holding down the Windows key and pressing E.

2 Towards the top of the Explorer window is a long bar that contains the path for the files or drives you're looking at. When you first open a new window, it says Computer. Click here and type ftp:// followed by your FTP server address. For example, you might enter "ftp://example. com". When you've finished typing your FTP address, press the Enter key. If you've done this before, Windows shows possible options in a menu below the box as you type. If your address is shown, you can click it instead:

Don't forget

Your homepage needs to have a special filename. It's usually index.htm or index.html. Your hosting company can tell you what it should be for your server.

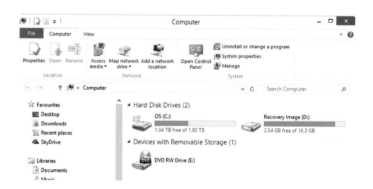

Hot tip

There are many dedicated FTP programs available, including FileZilla (**https://filezilla-project.org**) and CuteFTP (**www.cuteftp. com**). Website editors, including Dreamweaver and CoffeeCup HTML Editor, also provide a facility to upload files to your server.

3 Enter your username and password into the box and click the Log On button.

4 Your website will open in a Windows Explorer window. Depending on how your server is set up, you might see a number of different folders. You need to find the folder that contains your public website. For my server, I double-click the public folder and then double-click the www folder. Your hosting company can tell you which folder you need to upload your files into.

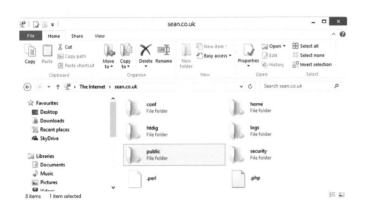

Don't delete any files or folders that your hosting company puts on your server, unless you understand what they do and know that removing them won't interfere with your website's operation.

5 Open a new Windows Explorer window containing your website files on your computer.

6 You can now use drag and drop to copy files and folders from your computer to your server, in the same way as you copy files between folders on your computer. You can select all the files in a folder by holding down the CTRL key and pressing A. Click on the selected files, move your mouse pointer to the server folder, and then release the mouse button. Windows will start to copy your files across. How long this takes depends on how fast your internet connection is, and the total size of the files you are copying. Don't forget to copy across all associated files, including images and style sheets, which might be in different folders to your HTML files.

Take special care not to overwrite the latest version on your PC with an old version from the server. To avoid confusion when copying from your PC to your server, I suggest you always arrange your PC window on the left and your server windows on the right.

7 Once your files have uploaded, test your site works by going to your internet browser and typing in your domain name. If you see your homepage, it's working!

After uploading a new file, test that web page in your browser to make sure it's worked okay. If you don't see a change, clear your browser cache and then try again.

If you're using a website editor, it will usually be able to update individual files for you on the server.

You can incorporate a blog in your website to enable you to easily add news stories or other updates later.

Updating your website

After your website has been uploaded to your server, you can easily make changes in future. You don't have to re-upload the entire website.

To modify the content of a particular web page, just edit its file on your computer. You can then upload that web page to your server and replace the old file there. If you want to add new images or web pages, you'll need to upload the files for those, and will probably need to replace some existing files to incorporate links to the new content.

Updating the look and feel

If you've designed your site using CSS (see Chapter 7), it should be easy to update the look and feel of your website by just uploading a new style sheet. When you replace a style sheet on your server, it will take immediate effect for all the pages that use it. You could dramatically transform the layout of your entire site by changing just one file on the server.

Have a fallback plan

Sometimes changes don't go quite as expected. Your site might use features that can't be tested on your computer, so that, for example, the style sheet looks messy on your real site when it goes live. It's a good idea to keep a copy of the previous working version of any file you're replacing. If you can't fix any problems quickly, you can then revert to the previous version.

You can keep this copy on your PC, or you can keep it on your web server. Before you upload a new version of main.css, for example, you could rename the existing version on your server to safe-main.css. If the new file doesn't work, delete it and rename safe-main.css back to main.css to restore the previous version.

When you are using Windows Explorer for FTP, you can rename or delete a file by right-clicking on it.

Avoiding content sprawl

As you add new sections to your website, keep an eye on folder structure. Your site will be easier to maintain if you organize pages that belong to the same section in a folder. If you keep adding content at the top level of the site (that is, outside of any folders), it will become difficult to find the files you need for maintenance.

15 Promoting your website

Getting people to visit your website is essential for making it successful. You can use SEO techniques or keyword advertising to come up in search engine results, plus many other ways to attract visitors to your site.

Introducing search results

For most websites, search engines are an essential source of visitors. They're the first place people turn to when they're looking for something specific online, and if that's something your website can offer them, you want the search engines to recommend your website. Without a good ranking in search engine results, your website can be close to invisible.

In this chapter, I'll share some key ideas that will help your site perform well in search engine results. First, you need to have an understanding of how search engines work and how people use them to find websites.

There are two parts to the Google search engine results:

● Down the right side, and in a lightly tinted box at the top, are adverts, triggered by the keywords you entered into the search engine. You can bid to place your adverts here using Google Adwords, which I'll cover later in this chapter.

● The rest of the page contains what are often called organic search results. This is Google's best guess at giving you links to the information you're searching for. Sometimes, it will be just a list of web pages. Other times, it will include images, videos or news stories. Google knows about over a trillion web pages, and the organic results are picked from these, based on Google's judgement of how well they match what you're looking for. No money changes hands, and you can't buy your way to the top of the organic search results. You can influence them, though, through careful design of your website and its content.

The practice of tweaking your website to help its content rank well in organic search results is called search engine optimization (SEO).

There are some SEO techniques that are based on tricking search engines or exploiting flaws in them. These "black hat SEO" techniques risk your website being banned altogether.

Microsoft's search engine Bing (www.bing.com) and Yahoo! (www.yahoo.com) use a similar results format to Google.

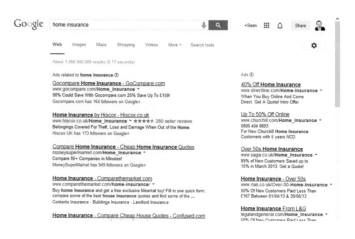

How people search

If somebody asked you to find a cheap flight to Spain, you probably wouldn't just type "flights" into Google. For most queries, people type in a few words so that they can more easily find what they're looking for, such as "cheap flights Spain". This is known as a key phrase.

Google will typically return millions of results, and tell you how many it's found at the top of the screen. At the bottom of the screen, there are controls for moving through the pages of results:

In practice, people rarely make it past the first few pages. If your site is ranked on page three of the search engine results, you might as well not be there at all. Many people won't even make it to page two. Instead, they will refine their search query by adding more words to it and searching again, making the search engine work smarter for them, instead of trawling through pages of semi-relevant results. These additional words are called "qualifiers".

The kinds of words they add include:

- Adjectives that better describe what they want

- Brand names for companies or products they especially want

- Location details, such as a country, town or city

- Details of a product type, such as "student discount flights"

- A verb indicating their intended action, such as "book flights" or "compare flights"

If you can use the same words on your website that people use to search, and put them in the right place on your site, you'll make it easy for Google to recommend your site when it thinks it might be the best result. Before you can do that, you need to research which words people are actually using.

Not all search phrases deliver equally valuable visitors. Those searching for "cheap" will be highly price sensitive, and so will be easily swayed by a rival's cheaper price. Those searching using words like "buy" are closer to making a purchase, and so might be more valuable to you.

213

People don't search for marketing guff. They search for products, places, people, benefits, content, and help (among other things). Think like a customer when you research your keywords.

Researching key phrases

The Google Adwords Keyword Planner shares some of Google's intelligence about the words and phrases that people use to search.

The tool is designed for Adwords customers, so they can optimize their paid-for listings. But it's free to use, and the results are equally applicable to organic SEO.

Don't forget

You will probably have different key phrases and qualifiers for the different pages on your website.

1 Go to **https://adwords.google.com/ko/ KeywordPlanner/Home**
Log in to your Google account, or create one.

Hot tip

Google Insights for Search (http://www. google.co.uk/insights/ search/) can show you the most popular search terms in different categories; enables you to compare how popular search terms are in different countries and towns; and shows you seasonal variations.

2 Click "Search for new keyword and ad group ideas".

3 Enter your product or service into the box, and add your product category, and/ or landing page, and/or product category. These are used to suggest keywords to you.

4 Click the Get ideas button.

...cont'd

5 Click the tab to view the keyword ideas.

6 The web page shows a table of suggested keywords. You can click one of the columns to sort the results by it.

Hot tip

If a key phrase has a lot of competition, it might not be worth trying to compete on it. It's better to identify niche phrases you can dominate, than to languish on page 20 of the search results for a highly popular phrase.

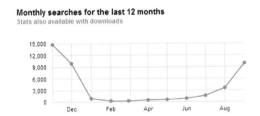

7 The average monthly searches tells you how many times a particular keyword is used on average. Click the graph icon beside it to see a trend graph, showing how the search volume changes over the year.

Monthly searches for the last 12 months
Stats also available with downloads

Hot tip

Try searching for things on Google to see what terms it recommends as you type. Many people will select one of these, even if they intended to type something else.

8 The competition column shows you how heavily contested these words or phrases are for advertising. It doesn't affect organic search results, but it is a good indication of how hard it might be to rank for a particular word or phrase.

9 Make a note of phrases that people frequently use to find your kind of content, but exclude any that are obviously too unspecific for your site to satisfy.

Beware

Sometimes the words that people use to search aren't the same words they want to read in your website content. Nobody wants to be greeted by a homepage that says "Welcome to our cheap hotel!"

Hot tip

If Google suggests your site in search results, and people rarely click it, Google will demote your site in its results.

Beware

If your article becomes little more than a list of keywords, search engines might ban you for trying to trick them. Focus on creating great content, and use these tips to give it its best chance of ranking.

Where to put search terms

Following keyword research and brainstorming, you should have a number of key phrases that apply across your site, and between five and ten qualifiers that might be used to fine-tune results.

You might have different key words and phrases that apply to different pages on your website. For example, you might have search terms that are specific to different product pages (perhaps even model numbers), as well as broader terms that you would like your homepage to rank against (such as "buy camera"). Search engines are not case sensitive, so don't worry about whether the terms appear in upper or lower case in your web pages.

Using search terms in headlines

If your website is correctly marked up using HTML, search engines can understand which bits of the page are headlines and will give the words in them more weight. Use your search terms in your headings, and make sure that your headings are correctly marked up using heading tags like <h1> (see Chapter 6).

Using search terms in your articles

You also need to scatter your search terms liberally throughout the main content of your web pages. Your primary key phrases should be used without any words splitting them up. You can distribute your qualifiers throughout the article, and should use variations wherever possible. For example, if you have an article about singing, use variants such as sing, sung, sang, sings, and singing.

Using search terms in your link text

The words in a text link are understood by Google to be a description of the page linked to. This applies even if the link is between two pages on your own website. It's a good idea to include a key phrase in your internal links, wherever possible.

Using search terms in your page title

There is an HTML tag that is used to mark up the title of a web page. This title doesn't appear as part of the web page content (unlike your headings), but it is shown in the title bar at the top of the browser window. It's also used as the bookmark name when somebody adds a page to their favorites.

Google uses the title tag as the text for its link to your site in its search engine results pages. A good title can encourage people to click through to your site.

...cont'd

You add your title between <title> and </title> tags in the header of your HTML document. You should keep your title tag to under 65 characters (including spaces), and include up to three of your most important key phrases. Make sure the title is useful to a human reader, and not just stuffed with search engine terms.

Using search terms in your description

You can feed search engines a description of your site to use in their search engine results, too. You use what's called a meta tag in your web page, which includes information about the page that doesn't normally appear in the web page content.

In your description meta tag, you have about 20 words to sell the benefits of your site, and encourage people to visit. Think back to the differentiators you created when planning your website. They will help you to write a description that sells the unique benefits of your website. Give each page a unique description, and make it specific to the web page.

Here's how you use the description meta tag:

```
<meta name="Description" content="Description goes here">
```

Below you can see example HTML from a web page that has a title tag and description meta tag. This is just an excerpt: there would typically be other code between the <head> and </head> tags too:

```
<head>
<title>Journalism Careers: careers and training advice for writers</title>
<meta name="Description" content="This site answers your questions about writing for magazines, journalism training, being a freelance journalist and much more to do with journalism careers.">
</head>
```

This is what that page looks like in the search engine results:

Journalism Careers - careers and training advice for writers ☆
This site answers your questions about writing for magazines, journalism training, being a freelance journalist and much more to do with **journalism careers**.
www.**journalismcareers**.com/ - Cached

When Google shows search results, it puts the terms the user searched for in bold. If these terms are in your title and description, it will draw the eye, and encourage people to visit your site.

There is also a keywords meta tag, but search engines give it little weight, if any. It has a similar syntax to the description meta tag and also belongs in the header of your page:

```
<meta name="Keywords" content="keyword1, keyword2, keyword3...">
```

7 top tips for SEO

Hot tip

The best way to get links is to create fantastic content that people want to link to.

1 One of the most influential factors for ranking your website is the number of links it has coming into it, and where those links come from. One-way links to your site (that is, links you don't reciprocate) are rated as more important, but it's still a good idea to exchange links with business partners, and others you trust. Don't swap links with spammy sites: if you get into a bad link neighbourhood, Google might penalize you. Only link to sites you're happy to recommend.

2 If you can get others to link to you, try to get them to use one of your desired search terms in their link text.

3 Avoid having content in your site that is duplicated, either elsewhere on your site or on another site.

4 Use descriptive names for the folders on your site and your filenames. If your editor automatically creates pages, with names like Page1.htm, change them to more descriptive names, such as buying-cameras.htm. Use a hyphen to separate any words in your file or folder names, and try to use some of your search terms here, too.

Beware

A link from one web page to another is usually seen by search engines as an endorsement of it, but sites can include a code in the link to say that it shouldn't be. This is typically used in blog comments and other places where people can submit their own links unchecked. Mark up any links you don't want to endorse with the nofollow attribute:

```
<a href="http://
www.example.com"
rel="nofollow">Link
text</a>
```

5 Make sure every page on your website can be reached through a simple HTML link. You can consider having a sitemap page which links to every other page, to make it easy for search engines to find all your web pages. Beware of using Flash or JavaScript for navigation, because search engines might struggle to follow it.

6 Update your site regularly. Google likes to see a site that is being regularly refreshed with new content. Having a blog can help.

7 Avoid overly long web pages. It's better to have ten pages of 400 words, than to have one page of 4,000 words. It gives you nine more opportunities to suggest page titles and descriptions to the search engine.

Submit your website

Search engines use programs called spiders to crawl the web: the program looks at a web page, follows the links in it, looks at that web page, and keeps crawling deeper into the web.

If you have links coming in to your website, search engines should be able to discover it naturally. However, you can help them to discover your website by submitting it to them directly.

You only need to give them your homepage, and they will follow the links from there. After you do this the first time, the spiders will revisit your website at regular intervals to see what new content you have published.

You can submit to Google at **http://www.google.com/addurl/** and to Bing at **http://www.bing.com/webmaster/SubmitSitePage.aspx**
Both are free. They only ask for your URL: everything else they will work out from the website itself, so make sure you have completed your search engine optimization first.

It's a good idea to see whether there are any directories that cover your industry or profession, by searching for "dentist directory" or something similar. Directories will sometimes provide a respected one-way link to improve your SEO, as well as referring their own traffic. Many directories charge for inclusion or for consideration, but for businesses this can be a good investment. There might also be directories of local businesses you can apply to be listed in, and directories specific to your type of work, such as design showcases.

Hot tip

The way that Google picks websites to show you (its search algorithm) is refreshed every few months. Your site might go up or down the rankings, depending on the new algorithm. Your ranking might also change as other sites compete to try to knock you off the top spot and the popularity of search terms changes. SEO is an ongoing part of managing a website. If you rest on your laurels, a rival site might well snatch them from you.

Using keyword advertising

If you can't get to the top of Google's organic search results, you can pay to advertise using Google Adwords (**https://adwords. google.com**). The advertising model is known as pay-per-click (PPC), because you only pay when somebody clicks on your advert to visit your website.

The process works like this:

Pay attention to your margin (how much you make on a sale) and your conversion rate (how many people clicking on your advert buy) to work out a sensible bid. There's not much point in paying more than you'll make in profit from that click.

1 You research your keywords. You can use the same keywords you use for your organic SEO, or can use different ones. You can research your keywords using the same Keyword Planner.

2 You create a campaign. An advertising campaign can include many different keywords and their related adverts, but they all have the same geographic and demographic targeting, and all share the same daily budget.

3 You create an ad group, which contains one or more adverts and a set of related keywords. Google is most closely associated with the text ads it pioneered, but you can also show image or video adverts. To create a text ad, just fill in the form. When your ad is shown on Google, any search terms that are in the ad will be bold, so consider using one of your keywords in the ad text. Your display URL should be just your domain name, so people can easily read and remember it. Your destination URL is where people go when they click on your ad (your "landing page"). Choose a page that matches your keywords

Microsoft's Bing has its own PPC system (http://advertise. bingads.microsoft. com/) and Facebook has a PPC system that enables you to select audience by location, age, and interests (www.facebook.com/ advertising).

well. There's not much point doing sophisticated targeting and then dumping everyone at your homepage.

4 Enter the keywords you want this advert to display against. You can enter sophisticated criteria, such as excluding certain terms (use a minus before the keyword), and showing the ad only for exact matches of the phrase or the whole search term (by putting it in square brackets). Google will suggest some keywords, which you can also include.

To pause a campaign, go to your Campaigns tab and click beside the campaign name.

5 Set your maximum cost per click (CPC). This is how much you're prepared to pay for one visitor to come to your website. It's not necessarily what you will pay. The bidding works in the same way as auction bids on eBay. You enter your maximum bid, but you'll only be charged as much as is necessary to beat the next highest bidder.

The Google Display Network can show your adverts on websites that participate in its Adsense program, including many hobbyist sites you couldn't hope to deal with directly. Google will show your ad when your keywords match a partner site's content. You can refine your targeting demographically, to reach certain age groups or genders.

6 Use the search traffic estimator to see how much the keyword and bid combination will cost you. You'll find it underneath the keywords box, but it only makes sense after you've added your bid details. When you're ready, save your campaign and it will go live.

7 Use the data Google provides on clickthrough rate and the position of your ads to refine your keywords, ad copy and budget. Keyword advertising is not a one-off activity: to really benefit, you need to continuously refine your campaign in line with the data.

Hot tip

If you're placing a Flash advert, you'll be asked to provide an image ad that can be used when Flash isn't available in the user's browser.

Hot tip

People often call this kind of advertising "banner advertising", but it includes a wide range of different advertising types and sizes today.,

Display advertising

If there's an existing website that reaches your target audience, you might be able to advertise on it. This is often called display advertising.

With pay-per-click advertising like Google Adwords, the risk is small, because if nobody comes to your website, you don't pay anything. Often, display adverts are charged per thousand impressions (cost per mille, or CPM for short), which means you pay for 1,000 people seeing the ad, even if nobody visits your website. And most people won't: clickthrough rates are typically around 0.1%, and only about 2.5% of people might interact with a Flash advert within the website hosting it. For big companies focused on brand impressions or campaigning organizations, who can communicate their whole message in an interactive ad, this form of advertising can be extremely valuable. If your goal is to drive people to your website, you'll need deep pockets, though.

If a website is geared up to accept paid adverts, it will usually have a media pack explaining the number of visitors the site gets, and roughly what kind of background those visitors have. The media pack will also list prices, although the price you actually pay often depends on how well you negotiate. Your advert will need to meet the website's guidelines (including a maximum file size, in some cases).

The Internet Advertising Bureau (**www.iabuk.net**) publishes guidelines for adverts and updates them as new advertising sizes and methods go in and out of fashion.

Hot tip

Often you can reuse your advert on different websites, because they use the same sized advertising space.

More promotion tips

It's not just about SEO and advertising. There are many other ways and places you could promote your site. You've probably thought of some already, but here are a few suggestions:

- **Email.** Add a plug for your website to your email signature, so that a short advert goes out with every email you send or reply to. It's an easy and automatic way to let your friends and acquaintances know about the site.

- **In your business.** Include your website address on your business cards, letters, vans, carrier bags, receipts. It's better if you can give people a good reason to visit, too, such as telling them they can print discount vouchers on the website.

- **Offline advertisements**. Buy adverts in magazines, shop windows or wherever else your potential visitors might be.

- **Newspapers and magazines**. Write a short press release explaining the who, what, why, how, when and where of your website, emphasizing benefits to visitors. Email it out to key journalists and magazines that cover your market (both on the web and in print), when the site launches.

- **Network.** Participate in forums, social networks, and blog commenting to connect with others who might like your website content. You can't just turn up and start advertising, but if you become a valued member of the community, people will notice you and your website. Many forums enable you to include a short signature on your posts, and social networks give you a profile where you can link to your website and explain what it does.

- **Create an affiliate program.** Affiliate programs enable you to pay websites for sending you paying customers. Amazon has pioneered this model with its associates program, which pays websites a commission on any sales referred through a link. Several intermediaries exist to help you set up your affiliate program, including Tradedoubler (**www.tradedoubler.com**), Linkshare (**www.linkshare.com**), and Commission Junction (**www.cj.com**).

- **Syndicate your content.** Enable other websites to embed your content, but don't let them just paste your articles in, otherwise Google might punish you for duplicate content.

For these tips to work, you should ideally have a memorable domain name, and be able to tell people about a clear benefit for them of visiting your website. You might be able to offer out-of-hours support, discounts, online ordering or exclusive content, for example.

223

Links aren't just beneficial for search engine rankings. A link in a prominent position on a busy website can bring you lots of visitors. The best link relationships come when somebody has a genuine desire to recommend your website, so focus on creating great content and building solid relationships, rather than begging strangers for links.

Hot tip

Airlines and rail operators often have their own apps that they promote from their websites. Using the app provides direct access to the information that's also on the website. Apps can help companies to develop a deeper relationship with customers, by giving them information in as convenient a way as possible.

Hot tip

It doesn't hurt to ask visitors to bookmark your site, too, although most bookmarks are like the content of filing cabinets: filed once, never seen again.

Above: The RSS logo

Bringing visitors back again

Visits to websites can be so fleeting, and people aren't very likely to buy something on their first visit. Even if somebody likes your website, there's no guarantee they'll remember to come back.

There are a few techniques you can use to promote repeat visits to those who discover your website.

- **Create an email newsletter**. People are defensive of their email inboxes, so don't intrude by sending unsolicited bulk emails. But you can ask website visitors and customers to join your newsletter (or "opt in"), so that you can keep them informed. Vertical Response (**www.verticalresponse.com**) offers an affordable system for managing lists and sending emails and provides a subscription form you can paste into your website.

Sign Up Today!

* required

First Name:

Last Name:

Email Address: *

Company Name:

Join Now

Email Marketing by VerticalResponse

- **Use Twitter**. Ask visitors to follow you, and use the site to keep your followers informed about new products and content on your website.

- **Create souvenirs**. If you can provide something that people will download and use, they'll have a reminder of your website on their PC. For example, you could create discreetly branded images for use as Windows wallpaper, a downloadable video or audio recording (often called a podcast), an app, or an ebook packed with helpful advice.

- **Use RSS**. Most content management systems and blogs can enable an RSS feed to be published. This is a specially formatted text file that contains your latest headlines and stories. People can use an RSS reader to watch RSS feeds from lots of websites in one place, which makes it easier for them to watch the latest stories across many sites.

16 Measuring success

Gather data about website visitors and how they use your site to help evolve your website design and content.

If you have spiders visiting your site that are consuming more bandwidth than you want, you can ask them not to visit part or all of your site. To do this, you create a robots.txt file. Wikipedia has a good introduction. Take care that you don't turn away a major search engine with a poorly configured robots.txt file.

Measuring visitor interaction

There are two different approaches you can use to measure how people use your website. One uses the server's record of the files it sent out (the server log), and the other uses JavaScript to identify human visitors. Both typically provide reports through a web interface, so you don't need to install any software. Neither approach is perfect, so it's best to use both together.

Using server logs

Your hosting company will usually provide statistics to you, which are based on your server logs. Keep a close eye on these, because the hosting company uses them to work out whether you're working within your allowed bandwidth, or whether they should charge you more!

The advantage of using server logs is that they can tell you which search engine spiders are visiting your site, what errors occurred (such as missing pages), and how your bandwidth is being used. You can use your server logs to identify files that account for a lot of your bandwidth, so that you can optimize the size of these files. That improves your website speed and could also save you money on your hosting bill. You can also measure downloads of non-HTML files, such as PDF files or MP3s, relatively accurately.

The disadvantage of using server logs is that they have no insight into what people actually do. The reporting tools make some clever guesses, but the tools often can't tell the difference between one long visit and two short ones. If somebody views a page from their browser's cache or from their ISP's cache, it won't show up in your stats at all. Some internet connections might look like one person in your logs, but could actually represent many hundreds or thousands of people.

Right: The AWStats software analyzes server logs to deliver a detailed report. You can download it for free at **http://awstats. sourceforge.net**, but something like this might be set up for you by your hosting company as part of the service it offers.

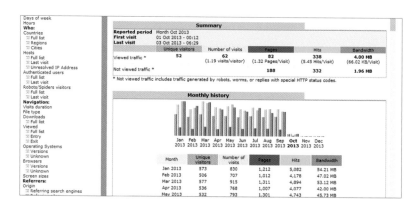

Using JavaScript tags

To get around the limitations of server log analysis, web analytics solutions were built that use JavaScript. Each web page has a small snippet of JavaScript code added into it, which is executed whenever the web page is loaded into the browser.

That code then tracks what visitors do on the web page, measuring the length of their visit and the path they take through the website. Web analytics solutions using JavaScript can even measure repeated views of web pages stored in a cache.

Although this provides much richer and more human data than server log analysis, it has its drawbacks. It won't work where JavaScript isn't supported (although that will be a tiny minority of visitors). The tag will have a small impact on the download time of your website (although it won't affect your bandwidth, because the JavaScript is stored on your analytics provider's server). The biggest challenge is that you have to add the tag to every page on your website. Some HTML editors will enable you to easily modify all your web pages at once, using templates or a site-wide search and replace. If your site uses a content management system, you can usually add the tag to your page template once.

There are lots of analytics solutions available. Google Analytics (**www.google.com/analytics**) is one of the most popular, and it's free, so it's well worth trying it out. Google Analytics uses graphs, maps and pie charts to help you identify trends and demographics. You can drill down into the numbers for more detail.

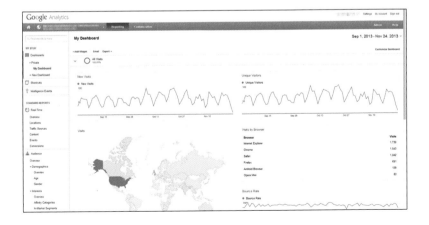

Web analytics is the term used to describe software that analyzes the behavior of website visitors.

Don't compare numbers from different analytics packages, because they will be based on slightly different assumptions.

Web analytics software uses cookies, which are small text files that the browser can store on the visitor's PC. Some people delete their cookies regularly, which will stop the analytics software identifying those repeat visitors.

Often the trends in the numbers are more useful than the absolute values. Don't fixate on your number of visitors, but do worry about whether they go up or down in the medium term. Expect to see fluctuations from month to month.

Don't forget to check your stats from time to time, to see how your site is performing. It's easy to forget, so why not put it in your diary for the end of each month?

The landing and exit pages are the pages where people arrive at and depart from your website.

What the numbers mean

People talk in hushed tones about "analysis paralysis": having so much data you don't know where to start. Analytics software can seem a bit daunting at first, but once you understand what the data means, you can easily focus on the most useful bits.

This is what the metrics represent:

- **Hits.** You'll see this in your server log stats, but you should largely ignore it. Every file download is a hit, so a web page with a style sheet and three pictures might be five hits. It tells you nothing about human behavior.

- **Bandwidth.** The total size of all the files your visitors downloaded, including automated visits from search engine spiders. Most hosting packages have a bandwidth limit.

- **Unique visitors.** The number of different people who visited your website. The software is fooled by people who use multiple browsers or computers, and by people who share a browser. But this metric remains the best indication of how many individuals visited your site.

- **Number of visits.** The number of different occasions on which people visited your site. This will include the total number of visits by regular visitors, as well as one-off visits by others.

- **Pages or page views.** The number of different web pages that were viewed.

- **Pages/visit.** The average number of pages viewed in a visit is a good way to measure how engaged your visitors are.

- **Average time on site.** In Google Analytics, this is measured in hours:minutes:seconds.

- **Bounce rate.** The percentage of people who arrived at one page and left your site at that same page. A high bounce rate might reflect poor navigation between pages on your site, might show that people didn't find what they wanted on your site, or might be a good thing if people are clicking on adverts to leave and you're being paid for that click.

- **New visits.** The percentage of people visiting the site that the analytics package doesn't recognize from a previous visit.

Other important metrics

The number of visitors on a website and how long they spend there are important metrics, but they're rarely an indicator of whether the site is meeting its objectives or not. Few sites are built purely to be looked at.

Think back to the purpose of your site, which you defined when you were planning it. What is the best way to benchmark your success? Ideally, you will have defined this at the start of the project, too. For example:

- If you want to improve customer service, measure how the website is affecting the number of returns, complaints or phone calls you receive. Survey customers to see whether they are more satisfied now than they were before.

- To see how your website is affecting your reputation, look at how many people link to your website and what they write about it. Research how often your web pages are recommended on sites like Facebook and Twitter.

- If you aim to sell, measure your total sales volume, value of sales per customer and number of customers. Consider any offline sales that are influenced by the website, where appropriate, too.

- Where it's important to build relationships, look at the number of email newsletter subscribers, RSS subscribers, registered members or Twitter followers you have.

- If you want to create a community or learn from your audience, then consider how many comments and forum postings your site attracts, and the quality of that user generated content.

You might need to introduce sophisticated tracking systems in your business to gather some of the information you need. For example, when customers phone up, ask them where they found your number and keep a record of it. If customers call up to complain, find out whether the website failed them or whether they didn't think to go there.

Often, you can't easily tell whether your site is meeting its goals or not. It all depends on how visitors react to it. The only sure way to find that out is to ask them.

Some analytics tools including Statcounter (**www.statcounter. com**) and Sitemeter (**www.sitemeter.com**) enable you to display a cumulative count of visitors to date on your web site. It can make your site look trivial, unless you've got some truly impressive numbers. Both tools also offer an option without a public counter.

If you use bit.ly (**http:// bit.ly**) to create a shortened version of a link, bit.ly will count each time your link is clicked. You can use this to measure the effectiveness of particular link placements. Search engines might not give you credit for links via bit.ly, though, so use it for isolated tests.

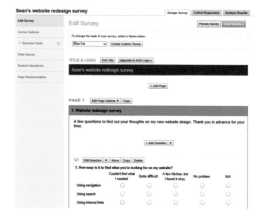

Creating a survey

The numbers are good for telling you what people do on your website, but they don't tell you much about why, or about how your visitors feel about your website experience. Find out with a quick survey from Survey Monkey (**www.surveymonkey.com**). Here's how to create one:

1 Create an account for Survey Monkey, if you don't already have one, or log in if you do. Click the button to create a survey and give it a descriptive name. Choose a category for your survey and click Continue. Click Edit Page and you can add a title and description for the page.

2 Click Add Question. You can choose from a number of question formats, including multiple choice, comment boxes and rating scales. The customization options you have will depend on the question you're asking. For a multiple choice question, you'll be prompted to enter the values for all the rows and columns, for example.

3 You can keep adding questions until you've finished. You can also add additional pages to the survey.

4 When you've finished creating the survey, click the tab to Collect Responses. Select the option to add the survey to your website. You can choose to embed it into your web page, or to have the survey or an invitation to complete it pop up when somebody visits your web page.

5 Copy the code provided and paste it into your web page. Test the survey works and publish your web page. To get your data, log in to your account.

Enabling evolution

Your analytics data is as close as you can get to looking over your visitors' shoulders while they surf your website. It's extremely valuable information, but only if you use it. Operating a website should be an iterative process, where you use what you learn to continuously refine your design and content.

When you know which pages and stories people are most interested in, and those they tend to ignore, you can take the guesswork out of creating new content that meets their needs. You can even see which search engine keywords delivered you most visitors, which provides a valuable insight into what people were looking for when they landed on your website.

Take a look at your referring sites, too, which are the sites that send you visitors through a link. The context of that link and the originating site gives you an idea of what people following it were expecting to find. Not all links are equal, so knowing which sites send you the most visitors is important, especially if you've paid for an advertisement and link on those sites.

When you design your site, you have to guess which devices, browsers and screen resolutions people will use to view your website. Your analytics and survey data can give you the facts, so you can ensure your site offers a good experience to your visitors.

As well as using your data to refine your design, you can use it to refine your online strategy. Imagine you're running a shop and it's not selling as much as you want it to, for example. By looking at your data, you can see whether you have an empty shop, or whether you have lots of visitors leaving empty handed. If you don't have enough visitors, web promotion is your priority. If you have plenty of people browsing, look at how you can improve your conversion of visitors into sales. Is the Buy button obvious enough? Can people use the navigation? Try a simple usability test to see where you can make improvements.

A website is never finished. There is always change in your business or market, or new content to share. Using a combination of web analytics, surveys and usability testing, you can ensure that you're not making changes for the sake of it, and that your website continuously evolves to more closely match what your audience wants, so that it achieves the purpose you defined when you started reading this book.

Hot tip

Make small, incremental changes to your design and measure their impact. If you make huge changes, it's hard to tell what's helped and what might have made things worse.

Don't forget

You might not be able to make a change that doubles sales. But you could make 100 small changes over time, each of which increases your sales by 1%.

Credits

About the author

Sean McManus has written for Internet Magazine, Internet Works, Business 2.0 and many more. He is the author of the books Scratch Programming in easy steps, Raspberry Pi For Dummies (co-authored), and iPad for the Older and Wiser (co-authored). Sean's websites (**www.sean.co.uk** and **www. wildmoodswings.co.uk**) have been featured editorially by The Times, The Daily Mirror, BBC Click and BBC Radio 2.

Disclaimer

This book is not endorsed by or connected with any organizations whose screenshots or products feature in it. This book may include brand names and trade marks and these remain the property of their respective owners, and are used here editorially and for the benefit of their owners. While every care has been taken in the preparation of this book, neither the author nor publisher can accept responsibility for any loss or damage caused by following guidance in this book. The website **www.example.com** is reserved for use in documentation and books and is not a real website.

Acknowledgements

Indexing and page layout into In Easy Steps style: Karen McManus.

Many thanks to the companies and individuals who helped with screenshots, research requests and suggestions. These include: Lee Brimelow (Flash platform evangelist at Adobe), Jon Lovatt (executive creative director at Fortune Cookie), Jan Golding (director at Yoyo Design), Kelvin McManus (director at The Internet Works UK), Clive Goodinson (Founder of Pixton Comics), Suzanne Miller (CoffeeCup Software), Sarah Rogers (Tourism Ireland), Charlotte Blatchford, Laura Bottom (sales coordinator at Optelec), Stu Nicholls (www.cssplay.co.uk), Brent Silby, Coen Grift, Cameron Adams, Meri at Dryicons, Daniel Bruce and Rob Bowen at .net Magazine, Constantin Weimar (WM Team), John Politowski, Simon Van Hauwermeiren, Ben Klemm, Jenny Legg (British Heart Foundation), Petr Stanicek, Scott McCloud, Ed Sanders, Janina Himmen (www.sp-studio.de), Andrew Campbell-Howes, Cat Smith, John Hartnup, Steve Wright, Kim Gilmour, Steve Walker, Sarah Power, Siobhan Curham, Tim Benson, Marlène Morazin.

You can find the links from this book, code examples, and other supporting resources at www.ineasysteps.com or on the author's website, at www.sean. co.uk

You can find more great books in the In Easy Steps series, at www.ineasysteps.com

See inside back cover.

If you enjoyed this book, please blog about it or write a review of it on your favorite online store. Thank you!

Index

M

N

O

P

Q

R

S

T